Leadership
Handbooks

O F

Practical
Theology

Contributors

General Editor
James D. Berkley

Consulting Editor
Paul E. Engle

Executive Editor
Marshall B. Shelley

Senior Copy Editor
Gary Wilde

Editorial Administrator
Bonnie Rice

Associate Copy Editors
Richard Doebler
David Goetz
Craig Brian Larson
Kevin D. Miller

Editorial Assistant
Cynthia Thomas

Writers

Gordon Aeschliman. Editor, *Prism*, Colfax, Washington.

Michael J. Anthony, Ph.D., Claremont Graduate School. Associate Professor of Christian Education, Talbot School of Theology, La Mirada, California.

Charles Arn, Ed.D., University of Southern California. President, Church Growth, Inc., Monrovia, California.

Win Arn, D.R.E., Eastern Baptist Seminary. President, L.I.F.E., Monrovia, California.

John Ashmen, B.S., Philadelphia College of Bible. Director of Member Services, Christian Camping International/USA, Colorado Springs, Colorado.

Myron Augsburger, Th.D., Union Theological Seminary (Richmond). President, Christian College Coalition, Washington, D.C.

Nancy D. Becker, M.Div., Union Theological Seminary (New York). Pastor, Ogden Dunes (Indiana) Presbyterian Church.

James D. Berkley, D.Min., Fuller Theological Seminary. Editor, YOUR CHURCH, Carol Stream, Illinois

Warren Bird, M.Div., Alliance Theological Seminary. Writer and editor, Suffern, New York.

Paul Borthwick, M.Div., Gordon-Conwell Theological Seminary. Minister of Missions, Grace Chapel, Lexington, Massachusetts.

Douglas J. Brouwer, D.Min., Princeton Theological Seminary. Senior Pastor, First Presbyterian Church of Wheaton, Illinois.

John A. Burgess, Ed.D., Harvard University. Professor of Education, Emeritus, Gordon College, Wenham, Massachusetts.

Andre Bustanoby, Th.M., Dallas Theological Seminary. Marriage and family therapist, Bowie, Maryland.

Kenneth W. Campbell, M.Div., Trinity Evangelical Divinity School. Director of Ministries, ACMC, Inc., Wheaton, Illinois.

Scott Campbell, Th.M., Boston University School of Theology. Senior Pastor, International Protestant Church, Brussels, Belgium.

Douglas M. Cecil, D.Min., Dallas Theological Seminary. Assistant Professor of Pastoral Ministries, Dallas Theological Seminary, Dallas, Texas.

Linwood H. Chamberlain, Jr., M.Div., Hamma School of Theology, Wittenberg University. Co-pastor, First Evangelical Lutheran Church, Lorain, Ohio.

Randy Christian, D.Min., Fuller Theological Seminary. Associate Minister, Adult Education and Family Ministry, Beaverton (Oregon) Christian Church.

John Cionca, Ph.D., Arizona State University. Associate Dean, Bethel Theological Seminary, St. Paul, Minnesota.

Lyman Coleman, S.T.B., Biblical Seminary in New York. Founder, Serendipity Foundation, Littleton, Colorado.

Gary R. Collins, Ph.D., Purdue University. Executive Director, American Association of Christian Counselors, Kildeer, Illinois.

Harvie M. Conn, Litt.D., Geneva College. Professor of Missions, Westminster Theological Seminary, Philadelphia, Pennsylvania.

Eleanor A. Daniel, Ph.D., University of Illinois. Professor of Christian Education, Cincinnati Bible College and Seminary, Cincinnati, Ohio.

Edward G. Dobson, Ed.D., University of Virginia. Senior Pastor, Calvary Church, Grand Rapids, Michigan.

Dave Dolan, M.P.H., University of the City of Los Angeles. Executive Director, Center for Ministry Resources, San Anselmo, California.

William Donahue, M.A., Dallas Theological Seminary. Director of Couples Ministry, Willow Creek Community Church, South Barrington, Illinois.

Brett Eastman, M.Div., Talbot School of Theology. Area Director of Small Groups, Willow Creek Community Church, South Barrington, Illinois.

James Andrew Edgren, D.Min., Wesley Theological Seminary. Director, Chaplain's Commission, National Association of Evangelicals, Washington, D.C.

Chris Ellerman, M.S.W., George Williams College. Executive Director, Outreach Community Ministries, Inc., Wheaton, Illinois.

Roger Razzari Elrod, M.A., California State University, Chico. Golden Gate Area Director, InterVarsity Christian Fellowship, San Jose, California.

Douglas Fagerstrom, M.C.E., Bethel Theological Seminary. Minister of Adults, Calvary Church, Grand Rapids, Michigan.

Mark Galli, M.Div., Fuller Theological Seminary. Managing Editor, CHRISTIAN HISTORY, Carol Stream, Illinois.

Carl F. George. Adjunct Professor, Fuller Theological Seminary, School of World Mission, Pasadena, California.

Eddy Gibbs, D.Min., Fuller Theological Seminary. Associate Rector for Discipleship, All Saints Church, Beverly Hills, California.

Peggy M. Gilbert, M.S., University of Bridgeport. Director of Migration Services, World Relief, NAE, Congers, New York.

Wayne L. Gordon, M.A., Northern Baptist Theological School. Pastor, Lawndale Community Church, Chicago, Illinois.

Michael P. Green, Ph.D., University of North Texas. Associate Professor, Moody Graduate School, Chicago, Illinois.

Gary Gulbranson, Ph.D., Loyola University. Senior Minister, Westminster Chapel, Bellevue, Washington.

Ronald T. Habermas, Ph.D., Michigan State University. McGee Professor of Biblical Studies, John Brown University, Siloam Springs, Arkansas.

David C. Hacker, M.Div., Church Divinity School of the Pacific. Executive Director, Emergency Food Bank, Stockton, California.

John D. Hambrick, M.Div., Fuller Theological Seminary. Assistant Pastor, American Church in London (England).

Richard R. Hammar, L.L.M., Harvard Law School. Attorney at Law, CPA, Springfield, Missouri.

Quentin L. Hand, Ph.D., Boston University. Pastoral Psychotherapist, The Key Pastoral Counseling Center, Huntsville, Alabama.

Tim Hansel, M.A., Stanford University. Founder, Summit Adventure, Bass Lake, California.

Archibald D. Hart, Ph.D., Fuller Theological Seminary. Professor of Pschology, Dean, Graduate School of Psychology, Fuller Theological Seminary, Pasadena, California.

Paul H. Heidebrecht, Ph.D., University of Illinois. Administrator, Immanuel Presbyterian Church, Warrenville, Illinois.

Roberta Hestenes, D.Min., Fuller Theological Seminary. President, Eastern College, St. Davids, Pennsylvania.

Dennis P. Hollinger, Ph.D., Drew University. Pastor, Washington Community Fellowship, Washington, D.C.

Michael Jinkins, Ph.D., University of Aberdeen, Scotland. Pastor, Brenham (Texas) Presbyterian Church.

Darrell W. Johnson, M.Div., Fuller Theological Seminary. Senior Pastor, Glendale (California) Presbyterian Church.

H. Deen Kaplan, M.Div., Gordon-Conwell Theological Seminary. Vice-President, Public Policy & International Networks, National Coalition Against Pornography, Washington, D.C.

D. James Kennedy, Ph.D., New York University, New York City. Senior Minister, Coral Ridge Presbyterian Church, Fort Lauderdale, Florida.

Jerry R. Kirk, D.L., Grove City College. President, National Coalition Against Pornography, Cincinnati, Ohio.

Ronald S. Kraybill, M.Div., Harvard Divinity School. Director of Training, Center for Intergroup Studies, Cape Town, South Africa.

Bruce Larson, D.D., Seattle Pacific University. Co-pastor, The Crystal Cathedral, Garden Grove, California.

Ann A. Letson, M.Div., Louisville Presbyterian Theological Seminary. Associate Director, Department of Pastoral Care, Spartansburg Regional Medical Center, Spartansburg, South Carolina.

Steve Levicoff, Ph.D., Union Institute. Lecturer, Institute on Religion and Law, Ambler, Pennsylvania.

Roy W. Lowrie, Jr., Ed.D., Temple University. Professor of Christian School Administration, Columbia Bible College and Seminary, Columbia, South Carolina.

Aubrey Malphurs, Th.D., Dallas Theological Seminary. Professor and Department Chairman of Field Education, Dallas Theological Seminary, Dallas, Texas.

Conrad Mandsager, B.A., Wartburg College. Director of Field Ministries, JAF Ministries, Agoura Hills, California.

who live with or love someone who has abused alcohol, single adults and others who are without jobs or in transition, adult children of alcoholics or dysfunctional families, single mothers, children of single parents, and those suffering from the effects of serious mental illness in the family.

● *Age-related groups.* Churches can also develop support groups based on age. For example, our church has Campus Safari, an annual outreach of our youth department. They rent a gym on a Sunday morning, and for weeks ahead of time, students from our church invite school friends, teachers, and administrators to come for a morning of competition among area schools.

Another program, Backyard Bible Clubs, reaches a younger age group. After many years of traditional daily vacation Bible school, we

---

divorce, a number of people in every community seek healing from broken relationships. Many churches find divorce-recovery workshops effective in reaching out to these people.

● *During a crisis event.* Death, injury, a job layoff, and other kinds of crises cause people to consider the big questions of life: What is the purpose of my life? Why do bad things happen to me? What do I do when I can't fix things on my own? Is there a God who cares about me? Where can I find others who will support me during this crisis?

● *During a time of hurt.* Today's younger generation is a hurting generation. Divorce, drugs, and various forms of abuse have taken an emotional toll. The growth of the support-group movement is a direct response to this open window of opportunity.

● *During a period of physical renewal.* The physical fitness revolution has created fitness centers and spas around the country. Many people are renewing their commitments to walking, jogging, or participating regularly in sports programs such as softball, volleyball, or basket-

ball. Churches can reach out to these unchurched folks through various sports-oriented programs.

● *During the transition to single parenting.* More people are single today than at any other time in the history of the United States. However, while singles are open to the gospel, singles ministry is more complex than simply offering a college and career Bible study as we did in the past. One of the windows open the widest today is that of ministry to new parents who are single. Such ministry may well offer spiritual-growth opportunities along with practical support and help for real-life problems.

● *During the child-care years.* The continuing need for two-income families produces the corresponding need for child care. Here is a window wide open to the unchurched.

Churches that respond to these and other open windows of opportunity will find their evangelism efforts blessed as "God gives the increase."

—*Gary L. McIntosh*

made a major change in our focus by taking our program out into the community. In August, we run about forty Backyard Bible Clubs the same week, multiplying the opportunities to reach unchurched children and their families because we are out where the needs are.

Whenever we can shift evangelism out of the walls of the church and into the community, we can be more effective in attracting special target groups among the unchurched.

Getting Started

No church can reach every potential target group. It's important, therefore, to develop a careful strategy that will accomplish the goal of evangelism with carefully selected target groups. Consider these crucial steps:

Urban Evangelism

In cities such as New York and Los Angeles, as many as a hundred different people groups live within two miles of one another. But the obstacles to reaching these nearby peoples are uniquely difficult. Many of the urban lost are crushed spirits with little hope for a better future for themselves or their children. Years of separation and neglect from the mainstream have raised high walls of distrust, anger, and blame.

The Mission Field Next Door

Reaching this difficult mission field for Christ must begin with a proper understanding of the gospel, which is the visible demonstration of God's love (see Luke 7:18–23). How do we strategically put the gospel into loving action among urban people? After thirty years of ministry among the poor, I believe we must recognize four key characteristics of effective urban evangelism as

we address the unique challenges of outreach within the mission field next door.

• *Effective urban evangelism is incarnational.* "The Word became flesh and dwelt among us" (John 1:14). Jesus did not commune in the morning, pass out tracts, and head back to heaven at night. Because Jesus identified with our sufferings, because he faced the same temptations we do, his teachings are trustworthy. Urban people are open to the gospel to the extent they trust the messenger, so people who have made the urban community their home do the most effective outreach.

The first step, then, to the most effective urban evangelism is *relocation.* While not all of us are called to go, churches must seek to build supply lines to those in the trenches of the urban community.

• *Effective urban evangelists are reconcilers.* If we were to go to China to reach the lost, we would learn the language, eat the food, learn all

Part II:

Missions

It was commanded by Jesus himself, yet finally begun as the result of a dire persecution. It was limited ethnically at first, before the doors were finally flung open wide to all peoples. It flourished under adversity and waned in prosperity. It was nearly abandoned for a time, later to be pursued vigorously—and then discouraged in some quarters.

It has taken the Good News to every continent, most peoples and tongues, and hundreds of millions of individual souls. It has brought nearly a third of the world's population—1.734 billion people, according to Operation World—to the point of calling Jesus Christ Lord and Savior.

It, of course, is missions.

Since the church as a whole has marching orders to "Go into all the world and make disciples," and since each local congregation has a part to play in obeying that order, the success of missions at all levels is of utmost importance. So how can missions best be accomplished? This is what concerns the writers of this section, just as it concerns conscientious church leaders and people called into missions, and just as it ultimately concerns the Lord of the Harvest. Here, then, are the suggestions these experienced leaders offer.

8

The Purpose of Missions

Christians traditionally have understood missions to include at least four broad purposes: the conversion of the lost, the establishment of the church, the restoration of the Creation, and the glorifying of God's grace throughout the universe forever. Yet some Christians today might question whether God has such a worldwide concern and whether he wants the church at large to develop the same cosmic perspective.

If so, we'll need to find ways to convince our church members that the living God is—and has been, since the advent of sin—a missionary God. He does yearn for all his creatures to offer him praise. By surveying key themes in the history of God's people, we will see that God constantly has called his people to labor for that great purpose with him.

God's Worldwide Concern

At first glance, the themes of the Old Testament may appear more parochial than universal in scope. Very quickly these Scriptures zero in on Abraham and the Semitic history of his descendants. God's grace seems to narrow down to Isaac and not Ishmael, to Jacob and not Esau. Yet, woven through the history of Genesis 1–11 are vivid reminders of a divine mercy whose interests are global.

• *The Genesis history and the unity of all humankind.* The story of Creation begins with a sweep that is worldwide in concern. This history, unlike the religious myths of the Ancient Near East, points to a cosmic sovereign, not a local deity. God's territorial dwelling place is not limited to a city-state like the Baals; the heavens and the earth are his domain (Ps. 24:1–2). Unlike the Babylonian creation account, this history gives us no hint of ethnic superiority for Israel based on a special creation relationship to an ethnic god. Likewise, the great assumption of the narrative is the unity of all humankind in the royal responsibilities of covenant imagehood before God (Gen. 1:26–27). This imagehood does not omit the startling inclusion of women, either from the act of Creation or from the creature's rebellion against the Creator.

The subsequent history of humanity chronicles the effects of this act of rebellion on a similarly universal scale. Alienation from God becomes incorrigible perverseness that can be halted only by the divine intervention of a universal flood. But after this flood judgment—and through it—God still remains faithful to his creation blessing to Adam (Gen. 1:28). He desires to fill the earth with a multitude of peoples (Gen. 9:1).

The Table of Nations in Genesis 10 reinforces this promise. Its link to the earlier history reminds us of God's postflood promise. And linking with the history subsequent to Babel, the Table looks forward to the return of these peoples to the redemptive fold through the blessing of the Semites in Abraham.

• *Abraham's call and the promise of worldwide blessing.* With the call to Abraham (Gen. 12:2–3), the same God who promises "I will make you into a great nation" promises "All peoples on earth will be blessed through you." The blessing of Abraham will one day "come to the Gentiles through Jesus Christ" (Gal. 3:14). All of this is the *beginning* of the restoration of the lost unity of humanity, not the *ending*. "Abraham is chosen, not just for his own glory, the good fortune of his descendants, or the misery of his enemies; rather, with him Yahweh begins a new chapter in the history of man. Abraham is the instrument for the salvation of the world" (Martin-Achard 1962, 35).

• *Israel's election and her testimony to the nations.* This same non-parochial perspective shapes the history of Israel as a witness to God's sovereignty among all nations. Israel's mission was to sanctify God's name before the peoples (Deut. 28:10). The preface to the constituting words of the theocracy speak of God's right of possession over all nations: "The whole earth is mine" (Exod. 19:5). In this light Israel is elected by God as "a kingdom of priests and a holy nation" (Exod. 19:6; 1 Pet. 2:9). She is to "fulfill a priestly role as a people in the midst of the nations. She is to represent God in the world of nations. What priests are for a people, Israel as a people is for the world" (Blauw 1962, 24). What kind of witness is Israel to be?

First, before the nations she testifies to God's covenant purposes. Her identity is shaped not by ties of blood or genealogy but by the electing grace of God (Deut. 26:18–19). The surrounding nations see themselves as incarnations of deity, their victories over other peoples being victories over others' gods. Israel's identity, however, comes only through obedience to the covenant God.

Second, before the nations Israel testifies to God's sovereign power. At Sinai the all-powerful God had promised victory over all those who would threaten his vassal, Israel (Exod. 23:22–23). In covenant power Yahweh keeps that word as the Israelites possess the land. Pagan treaties of that day called on the gods to bear witness to the secular ruler's faithfulness; in God's covenant the nations are to bear witness to the power of God (Lev. 26:45; Josh. 2:10; Ezek. 5:8, 14).

Third, before the nations Israel testifies also to God's mercy. Formed out of a "mixed multitude" (Exod. 12:38, KJ), she finds room for a Rahab and a Moabite Ruth in her community. A widow in Sidon and a Syrian leper named Naaman become harbingers of God's healing for the nations (Luke 4:25–28). Israel's laws extend equally to Israelite and to resident alien, the stranger in her midst (Lev. 19:10, 34; Num. 9:14; Deut. 24:19).

Fourth, before the nations Israel testifies to God's justice. The nations around her constantly exhibited oppression and injustice; righteousness was defined as "doing your own thing," or "having your own way." Israel was to model God's new charter of reality, righteousness as the companion of justice (Jer. 9:24; Amos 5:24). Quite uniquely, the poor were to be protected, not exploited in this display of justice (Deut. 10:17–18). A wise Solomon "administers justice" (1 Kings 3:28), and even the pagan queen of Sheba marvels (1 Kings 10:4, 6–7).

● *Israel's apostasy and the gathering of all peoples.* Against this background, Israel's failure to maintain her distinctiveness before God becomes a failure to enact her role as witness before the nations. In idolatry she "plays the harlot" with the very peoples before whom she was to model covenant holiness. A notable sign of this syncretism is the oppression of the righteous poor (Amos 2:6–7; 5:12).

In the face of Israel's acceptance of the lifestyle of the nations, the prophets call on those same nations to execute the other responsibility of the covenant witness (Deut. 17:7). Assyria and Babylon now serve as the Lord's instruments to administer the curses of the covenant (Hos. 10:10; Amos 6:14). Dispersion and exile for the twelve tribes become the judgment for disobedience.

Alongside the message of God's wrath against Israel, there is also a renewed promise of God's grace, to be shared this time by the nations. "The last days" are approaching, when God will come to be King over all the earth (Zech. 14:9). Israel will taste again the mercies of God, and the nations will spontaneously come to the Lord (Zech. 8:23). Jerusalem will be the gathering place of a new Israel, its citizens drawn from its former enemies (Ps. 87:4–6; Isa. 56:3–8). It will be a

dates who are looking for local-church support. Churches are welcome to invite these candidates to come and speak and to present their needs. At that time, church leaders can interview them and ask them to stay in the homes of church members.

What should the church look for in the people it intends to send to the field? Here are some things to inquire about and evaluate:

• *Spiritual maturity.* Candidates should reflect a warm walk in faith with Jesus Christ. The mark of God's hand upon their lives, their families, and their ministries should be clearly evident.

• *Current ministry involvement.* Are candidates using their spiritual gifts right now? Whatever they propose to do overseas should match what they are doing now: Helping people come to faith in Christ, teaching Bible classes, helping new Christians to grow, pitching in with work projects, caring for hurting people, counseling, helping neighbors, visiting shut-ins, and so on.

• *Academic qualifications.* Requirements vary according to ministry and mission board stipulations. Apart from specialized training, candidates should at least have a thorough grounding in biblical studies, theology, missions, anthropology, and linguistics. Language-acquisition aptitudes can be tested in advance.

• *Doctrinal compatibility.* Each church should make sure its missionaries agree with the church's theological perspectives. Again, depending on the church's stance, there may be some room for variance on certain issues. For instance, how important are eschatological views for the missionary teaching English as a second language in Russia?

• *Personal integrity.* Candidates for missionary service should be able to show that honesty, truthfulness, and integrity have marked their lives.

• *Missionary vision.* Missionaries should be able to explain why they want to serve overseas and how God has led them in that direction. What do they hope to accomplish for God? What are the biblical roots of their convictions?

• *Positive peer evaluation.* Again, character is the issue. Others ought to be able to testify to the potential missionary's commitment to Christ and to godly living.

• *Commitment to the church.* The church is the proving ground for service in God's kingdom. Out of a vital church life come prayer and financial support. If the candidate came to faith in Christ later in life, without roots in a local church, the church may well require one or two years of service and fellowship within a local congregation.

• *Sacrificial spirit.* Sacrifice is at the heart of missions, and the overriding spirit of missionary service is that of a servant. Would-be missionaries need to show this spirit before they leave for the field. A church can only gauge the willingness to sacrifice if there is time to develop a strong relationship with the potential missionary in the context of practical ministry work.

• *Healthy family life.* Many new missionaries carry scars from previous family problems. Churches and boards need to probe candidates' past histories frankly and find out what is being done to maintain strong marriage and family relationships. In some cases, church leaders will ask candidates to spend some time in counseling. Churches cannot assume that just because people want to be missionaries, they have solid marriages and families.

• *Willingness to grow home-based partners.* Although financial-support policies vary from board to board, all of them insist that their missionaries build a strong prayer-support team at home. Therefore, the church should encourage new missionaries to build strong relationships among the people in all their supporting churches.

Roles of Missionaries

Jesus told his disciples to go into the world and make disciples of all nations. This may sound like a singular task, but if we imagine missionaries all doing the same thing, we are mistaken. Most missionaries would say they are trying to glorify God by witnessing to the life-changing power of Jesus Christ. The God they serve, however, is a God of great variety.

A Diversified Ministry

Far from acting out the old stereotyped image of pith-helmeted, khaki-shorts-clad workers marching through swamps, today's missionary may be found doing mime on the streets of Amsterdam or showing the *Jesus* film in Uzbekistan. He or she may be producing radio programs that will air around the world from superpower stations as widely scattered as Ecuador, Monte Carlo, or the Seychelles Islands.

Plenty of rural workers are still needed, but even in remotest Irian Jaya, a translator's face may be lit by the glow of a computer screen. High tech and a close touch often characterize missionary work today. A relief worker in Somalia cradles a feverish, dehydrated baby and administers the latest antibiotic, while worlds away another teaches English to Japanese university students in a totally different environment.

Contrast and variety mark what missionaries do today, yet each one tries to apply an age-old gospel message with the latest technology that fits the situation.

A Biblical Impetus

Can all these various roles be traced to the Bible? Certainly! Consider the apostle Paul's ministry as an example. Paul said his main aim was to preach the gospel to those who had never heard it. Such groups are called *unreached peoples*. Stretching beyond our existing limits to reach them must be a priority

Throughout the process of preparation, application, and approval, the church seeks to build strong ties with its missionaries before they go overseas. Some require a year or two of internship on the staff, or in the pastorate, or with some form of home-based ministry among students, internationals, or the urban poor, for example. The goal is to assure that once the missionaries leave, they will be more than just a name on the church's support list or a picture on the world map.

Providing Support

Churches provide missionary support in various ways. Traditionally, missions giving is lumped under "benevolences" and assigned to the denomination's budget. Even so, it helps if the church receives current reports from the field, disseminates those reports from the

---

focus today. It is the only basis on which we can finish the task of world evangelization. Yet we can have focus and balance at the same time. Paul also taught *newly reached peoples* in person and through his epistles.

Paul reached out to *misled people*, too: those who had their Scriptures, leaders, and meeting places but no spiritual reality. They were the Jews. In our time, these misled people may be nominal Christians, of which there are vast numbers in Europe, Latin America, Africa, and North America.

In addition to these ministry targets, Paul was involved with helping *unfed peoples*. He conducted an ongoing relief program for famine-plagued Palestinians, demonstrating that this kind of work is truly a part of missionary endeavor. Paul was a man of both focus and balance, and that's what's needed on the mission field today.

A Challenging Future

Missionaries at the end of the twentieth century face a wide spectrum of needs among over 6,000 language groups. They will continue to evangelize, train leaders, establish churches, and distribute Bibles and Christian literature, yet new challenges will bring new roles for missionaries.

For example, who would have dreamed that with the collapse of Marxism around the world, missionaries would be asked to provide educational systems to impart Christian values and morality to entire nations?

Churches now support missionaries doing a wide range of ministries. This means there is a place of service for a variety of people in any given congregation. Some tasks can be done in a matter of weeks; some on a short-term basis of one or two years. Still others call for a lifetime commitment.

Variety of roles means breadth of opportunity. The task of the Christian missionary, then, is to keep the single gospel message central while meeting multifaceted needs with a variety of methods.

—Michael Pocock

pulpit and in Sunday school classes, and makes sure the missionaries are prayed for regularly. People will respond to these needs if the information they receive is fresh and personal.

As noted above, many churches build their own missions budgets around support for missionaries, missions projects, and relief and development needs. It helps if a special committee looks at these needs and then promotes them effectively, so the people can tie their giving to specific people and projects. When new missionaries are invited and need support, their needs can be considered as well, so that the church's missions giving increases annually. At the same time, the missions budget should be increased annually for each missionary to keep pace with inflation and to insure that these workers do not have to return from the field with deficit accounts.

Deputation and Furlough

Deputation is the time-honored word for what missionaries do to raise financial and prayer support prior to going to the field. *Furlough* refers to the year in which missionaries return home, usually every three or four years, to report back to their supporting churches and agencies. Supporting congregations need to consider carefully their role with and ministry to missionaries who are either raising funds in preparation for the field or returning home on furlough.

Help with Deputation

Once a missionary candidate is appointed by a board, the board assigns specific sums to be raised, usually in two categories: monthly support and outbound, or launch, funds. (Missionaries who belong to denominations that pool funds from local-church missions budgets do not have to travel among churches to raise individual support.) Many missionaries spend one or more years raising sufficient funds to go overseas.

Churches can help these people in many ways. For example, the congregation can: (1) Take on a significant amount of the support initially, either by drawing from the church's missions budget or by asking individuals to contribute; (2) provide housing, transportation, jobs, and child care while missionaries are on deputation; and (3) offer the names of other churches and individuals who would be likely prospects for the missionaries to visit.

Deputation is a time of intense faith stretching. Missionaries doing deputation work need much encouragement and prayer during these months or years. They must be delivered from feeling like beggars as they go from church to church raising funds for the worthy purposes of kingdom work around the world.

Some churches also encourage their members to take on additional support of missionaries beyond the church's budget. So when missionaries are invited to come and present their work and their needs, they may receive not only support from the church but from specific individuals as well.

Beyond building financial support, the church must also work to develop daily prayer support for its missionaries. Of course, prayer for missionaries must be included at the worship services and mid-week services, as well as in men's, women's, and youth prayer circles. Missionary prayer cards and letters work well for this purpose. Many churches also establish telephone hookups with missionaries during regular services in order to receive fresh news from the field. In addition, members may divide up the responsibility for writing to each

---

Furlough Encouragement

Furlough is now often called the "home ministry assignment," because some mission boards think "furlough" sounds too much like scheduled relaxation. Missionaries do have heavy responsibilities during furlough. They need to arrange for physical check-ups. They must find housing, transportation, and schools for their children. They will attempt to visit all of their supporting churches. If their support funds have fallen behind or the cost of living has gone up where they serve, they have to raise more money.

Many missionary families find the furlough experience particularly demanding and draining as they begin readjusting to life back home. Churches can help alleviate some of this stress in a number of ways. Consider these suggestions:

• *Offer free housing.* Some churches keep apartments and houses available for their missionaries. In other places, special agencies do this.

• *Provide transportation and clothing.* Missionaries coming from tropical climates will need warm clothing if they furlough in the north. Church families often have a spare car that missionaries can use.

• *Set up meetings.* Be sure the missionaries have one or more meetings with church leaders to give them firsthand reports. The missionaries should also be able to schedule informal times in the homes of various church members. As soon as possible, the missionaries should be given prime time to speak to the entire congregation and answer questions.

• *Plan and conduct review sessions.* Church leaders should review the missionaries' work over their last term and discuss their goals and assignments for the next term. It's also important to review future support needs. The missionaries may also need guidance from the church as they think through their next steps, in consultation with their sending board.

• *Encourage down time.* Hard workers need rest! The church might want to pay for a vacation somewhere. If the missionaries desire some refresher courses, the church can offer to pay the tuition.
—*James W. Reapsome*

missionary at least once a month. Sending quarterly "care packages" and special remembrances at birthdays and anniversaries brings added encouragement to overseas workers. Of course, as time and finances permit, church leaders should visit their missionaries on the field. Church members who travel overseas on business or vacations might also include visits to missionaries.

Evaluating Missions Agencies

To be effective and to exercise wise stewardship, the church needs to look not only at its missionaries' financial packages. The church must also evaluate the actual ministries to be carried out and the agencies with which the missionaries wish to serve. One of the best ways to begin mission-agency evaluation is to determine if the agency belongs to one of the major associations of mission boards: either the Evangelical Fellowship of Mission Agencies or the Interdenominational Foreign Mission Associations. These associations require stiff entrance tests for members and keep them maintaining high standards. Of course, not all reputable boards belong to these groups, for one reason or another. Another association giving financial credibility to charitable organizations is the Evangelical Council for Financial Accountability. A complete directory of mission agencies is published by MARC Publications (919 W. Huntington Drive, Monrovia, CA 91016).

Of course, it is important that the church invite someone from the mission to come for a visit and to bring all the necessary documents: financial audits, doctrinal statements, annual and five-year goals, reports from the field, the board's principles and practices, and names and addresses of other supporting churches. At this time the church can also go over the board's proposed support package for the missionaries, so that every dollar is accounted for. The church should also be clear about ministry assignments, conditions on the field, supervision on the field, and annual evaluations. For example, the church should expect a report of progress after the first year of language school.

The church and its missionaries should also look at strategic needs around the world. Simply because some people volunteer to work overseas and pass all the mission board's requirements does not necessarily mean the church should line up for support. For example, some countries are overloaded with missionaries, while others have relatively few Christian workers. Hundreds of tribal groups have no witness at all.

The church should also seek a balance in missionary vocations, too. Relatively few people volunteer to do pioneer evangelism and church planting, compared to the number who want to work at discipleship, church development, teaching, and so on. The task of training believers seems to attract more people than the challenge of starting new churches, either in urban high-rises or jungle villages. Since the church sees world missions as partnership, it should raise questions about assignments and about working with existing churches and the new mission agencies springing up overseas.

To get a feel for needs and opportunities around the world, a church might ask specialists to do research on both agencies and countries. Choose a number of agencies and ask to receive their magazines. Write to denominational headquarters for information. If the church is near a Christian college or seminary, the library will have numerous missions periodicals. The Evangelical Missions Information Service (Box 794, Wheaton, IL 60189) publishes *Evangelical Missions Quarterly* and *World Pulse Newsletters* to help churches and missionaries stay abreast of trends and needs.

Many churches gain valuable information and help from an organization called Advancing Churches in Missions Commitment (Box ACMC, Wheaton, IL 60189). This group publishes an excellent series of handbooks designed to help churches develop a vital missions program. It also sponsors regional training conferences across the country, encouraging churches with strong missions programs to help neighbor churches just getting started. Another organization devoted to helping churches start and maintain vital missions programs is World Thrust (Box 450105, Atlanta, GA 30345).

World evangelization is nothing if it is not partnership. Churches will find that most agencies are eager to help them launch successful, satisfying missionary-sending and support programs. Churches, missionaries, and boards are not antagonists. During their years of preparation and training, most missionaries begin to develop specific ministry goals and discover certain affinities for countries and people groups. They also begin to explore agencies that seem to offer both doctrinal and ministry compatibilities.

Here's a summary of what to look for in a mission board:

● *Doctrinal harmony.* Examine the published doctrinal statement carefully. Be sure it fits with the church's overall convictions. While talking with mission-board representatives and member missionaries, determine whether the agency is broad or narrow in its doctrinal convictions. Does it require strong internal consistency on such things as baptism, eschatology, church government, and relations with other churches and missions? Or does it have a broad latitude of acceptance?

An agency may say it is interdenominational, but over the years it may have developed some firmly held convictions that closely resemble those of a particular denomination. Ask what churches and denominations are represented among its missionaries. Ask what traditions have been elevated to doctrines. Read books and articles written by the board's leaders.

• *Compatible goals and policies.* Find out what the mission's purposes are. Why does it exist? What is it trying to accomplish? How well has it reached its own goals?

After examining both short- and long-range goals, decide if the emerging destination is where your church wants to go. Would the church risk everything to reach those goals? Do the church's goals, temperament, and ethos fit those of the mission board?

Ask whether the mission periodically reexamines its purposes and goals. Is there a regular review process in place? What new goals and strategies have appeared recently to show that the mission adapts to changes overseas and at home?

After hearing about policy positions, ask deeper questions about items the church doesn't agree with or understand. Such questions might relate to financial-support policies, field administration, agency government, rules of conduct, children's education provisions, health insurance administration, retirement practices, housing provisions, or furlough procedures.

Some boards are quite authoritarian, others less strict. Churches should try to find the best fit for their missionaries, as they assess candidates' gifts and temperaments. Church leaders should not give in to missionaries who want to work with a mission board that the church does not totally agree with, just for the sake of getting someone overseas.

• *A broad vision.* Does the mission's planning approach reflect creativity? Do the leaders constantly search for new ways to become more effective? Or does this agency give the impression of being tied only to traditional ways of doing things? The sending church should look for fresh ideas and broad vision, for "new worlds to conquer" enthusiasm.

• *Significant past accomplishments.* As the church's missionaries head for a specific field and ministry, they should look for the mission's track record there. Are the people already on that field encouraged by what has already happened, or are they giving up and coming home? Does the field show evidence of the Holy Spirit at work in measurable terms?

The church needs to ask about relationships and partnerships on the field among missionaries, between missionaries and the national church, and between the mission and other missions, home and international. Do these relationships reflect harmony or contention?

• *Agreeable lifestyle perspectives.* Probably the most difficult matter to probe is the mission's general attitude toward lifestyle issues. This attitude is shaped over the years by the agency's veterans, and it grows around unwritten codes. Key questions to ask are: Does the

committee needs to describe in detail your basic child-care policies, the services to be provided, the available transportation options, the facility to be used, and the job descriptions and qualifications of staff members. Include a plan to evaluate the program, as well.

• *Do a feasibility study.* The feasibility study should raise and answer key critical questions: Is the facility available? Does it meet program requirements, and is zoning approved? Are staff and volunteers ready to begin? Will our financial prospects provide the income necessary to meet expenses? The answers to these and other questions will either move the plan forward or force the committee to reevaluate and change the plan, based on available resources.

• *Implement the plan.* If the program is ready for implementation, a management committee needs to be commissioned and a director secured. From this point forward, the director implements the program with all the financial and personnel resources at his or her disposal.

—Chris Ellerman

Substance Abuse

Victims of substance abuse are among us in the church. Many such people, feeling trapped, wounded, and ashamed, are waiting for an outstretched hand from their pastors and other church members. When a wise pastor and compassionate congregation recognize that a primary duty is to bear the burdens of their struggling brothers and sisters, they will stretch out their hands with the offer of Christ's healing power.

Filling the Emptiness

A substance-abuse ministry can be one of the most gratifying and effective programs in the church's outreach plan, because it speaks directly to the emptiness of soul that Jesus came to fill when he promised us "abundant life" (see John 10:10).

Here are some suggestions for reaching out to those who have tried to fill that emptiness with mind-numbing chemicals.

• *Confront congregational denial.* It is surprising how little awareness of substance abuse many congregations have. Because of addiction's hallmark—denial—it is so easy for congregations, like individuals, to cry, "No addiction here!" Yet forms of substance abuse exist within virtually every congregation.

In some appropriate way, then, we must let the congregation know the leadership of the church is launching a new program to meet a newly recognized need. We can gently inform the people that a raging problem in our society will be addressed by this congregation and invite them to participate. We should approach this ministry as we would look after other hurts that call for the Lord's healing.

• *Thoroughly educate the volunteers.* Expert training for ministry volunteers is a must. Search the community's resources for agencies and individuals who are thoroughly equipped to provide education to members who will guide this new ministry. At the least, volunteers must know what addiction is, where it comes from, what the addictive personality is like, how to recognize symptoms, and how to teach family members about the destructive effects of enabling and co-dependency.

• *Take a holistic approach.* We minister best when we address all the victim's problems together—the physical and mental as well as the spiritual. We should make full use of the Christian Twelve-Step Program and its *Serenity Bible.* Also, most large cities have a Council on Alcoholism and/or a Drug Education Center. Agencies like these can provide excellent resources.

• *Team with other churches.* Church members must bear one another's burdens in this ministry. Since the ravages of addiction in our day comprise one of the weightiest burdens in history, whole congregations can increase their effectiveness in ministry by working together. In Charlotte, North Carolina, for example, churches have formed a Ministry of Recovery, which has encouraged several churches to collaborate in this vital Christian enterprise.

• *Recognize the ultimate source of all healing.* The eleventh chapter of the Gospel of John captures the clearest picture of Christian rehabilitation when the victory giver, Jesus, calls to the one in bondage to death: "Lazarus, come forth!" Then Jesus instructs his helpers to loose Lazarus from the graveclothes.

In light of Christ's vivid demonstration of his power to release from bondage, we might say an explicitly Christian treatment approach involves two basic steps: (1) introducing the addicted to the Great Physician and (2) helping them remove their "graveclothes"—the remnants of the old lifestyle.

In my own dark years of being hooked on drugs, I came under the care of several psychiatrists, two private sanitariums, and many other forms of treatment. Each medical professional and therapy gave valuable help and support, but my rescue ultimately depended on the love and grace of my healing Lord.

—*Gordon Weekley*

Prison Ministry

Prisoners often go unnoticed by the general church population. However, Jesus spoke about extending ministry to his followers who may be imprisoned (Matt. 25: 31–46). In fact, he said that showing compassion to those who are hungry, thirsty, or imprisoned is showing compassion to him. The writer of Hebrews also reminds us to pray for those in prison as if we are there with them (Heb. 13:3).

All a church needs to begin a prison ministry is two or three Christians who have a heart for those incarcerated. These Christians can arrange times to meet together to begin praying specifically for inmates and their families. From that point, the church can plan a quality ministry representative of our great Lord and King.

Planning the Ministry

Here are some suggestions for beginning and conducting prison ministries:

• *Go first as a guest* with an established ministry group. This helps a group gain experience and decide on the type of ministry they may be able to provide. Churches often serve by offering a Bible class, holding a short worship service, or counseling with individuals.

• *Meet with the chaplain and other prison officials.* It is important to explain ministry goals, learn the institution's requirements, and gain permission to begin. This is a good time to arrange a given time each week for visitation.

• *Use the Scriptures as the central focus.* Since rehabilitation — a change of heart—is one of the major purposes for the incarceration of law offenders, the Word of God is our greatest tool for prison ministry (Acts 2:37; Rom. 1:16; Heb. 4:12). Prisoners are not excluded from the gospel message; nevertheless, some, like Jonah, must be captured by God before they learn to accept it.

• *Visit frequently.* Most prison officials agree that frequent visits from the Christian community help improve inmates' behavior. Since prisoners are used to having their days highly structured and regulated, visitors need to be prompt and consistent with their scheduling.

Wise Practices

Seasoned visitors learn to be prepared for a few problems. Here are some dos and don'ts in response to the inevitable problems:

• Don't be discouraged by either small attendance or little verbal response. Few inmates are church oriented, and the results of our work may not be obvious in terms of radically changed lifestyles. However, the visitor and many others will be blessed by the ministry, and God's kingdom will increase.

• Don't be surprised by shallow professions. Some inmates use a profession of faith as a method of gaining special favors. It's best to just keep assuring inmates of God's impartial love and his complete forgiveness. This involves being patient and refusing to try to force decisions. We may only plant the seed; God may call someone else to be the harvester (see 1 Cor. 3:5–8).

• Do prepare for criticism at home. It's wise to secure enthusiastic support from the church leadership before starting a ministry. One big reason is that some inmates, upon release, may begin attending the church. Since a few members may feel uncomfortable with former inmates sitting next to them, a united church leadership can best deal with criticism of outreach to these unpopular folks.

• Do set up a support system for ex-convicts. The sad fact is that many released convicts eventually return to prison, and it's good to plan how to prevent that occurrence from the first day of a prisoner's release. Effective approaches get released prisoners involved with others in clear, consistent forms of accountability.

—James E. Martin

Helping People with Disabilities

Just as Jesus ministered to the whole person, we are called to care for the physical as well as spiritual needs of people. For people with disabilities, this coupling of the spiritual and the physical is essential if we truly are to make a difference in their lives.

Where Do We Start?

As we look to minister to those with disabilities, a few practical steps can get help us begin:

• *Conduct a survey.* Often, a church is unaware of who has disabilities in the congregation or community. Develop a survey to determine who is coping with a disability and what that disability is.

• *Develop a strategy for outreach.* Few people with disabilities attend church (about 1 in 20). Yet it is estimated that 10 to 17 percent of any given community is disabled. Many would attend church if they were invited and made to feel welcome. A team of volunteers can be assembled for outreach and ministry to those with disabilities.

• *Don't forget the family.* Often families are the primary caretakers of a person with a disability. Stress takes its toll on these families, as seen in their unusually high divorce rates (over 85 percent) and incidents of physical, emotional, and sexual abuse. Alienation from church and community are common in these families. A night out or an offer to do the grocery shopping can be a welcome relief.

• *Support the ministry from the pulpit.* This is not a ministry that can survive without support from the pastor. It's tough and unpopular. A pastor who promotes and models a warm response to people with disabilities will gain the congregation's support.

• *Start with disability awareness.* Even with a committed pastor, a team of trained volunteers, and an accessible building, the church may not be a pleasing environment for disabled people and their families. Recent studies indicate that "attitudinal accessibility" is more critical than physical accessibility. Planning a Disability-Awareness Sunday and using a disability-awareness study guide, such as *Hearts in Motion* (Agoura Hills, Cal.: JAF Ministries), can help the congregation understand the disability world and what the Christian's response should be.

• *Create an annual ministry plan.* The plan should reflect goals and objectives for the year. Avoid focusing on a single disability, as it tends to exclude people with other disabilities. Instead, build a ministry that crosses disability lines, such as respite care and support groups. The plan should promote inclusion, which simply means participation in the usual activities of the able-bodied community. The only real need for segregating any disability group is for educating those with mental retardation.

Tips for Workers

In fostering the personal side of the ministry, we should observe certain relationship principles:

- When meeting a person with a disability for the first time, treat that person like you would any other person you might meet.
- Establish eye contact when speaking with the disabled person.
- Ask questions regarding the disability when appropriate, not out of morbid curiosity.
- Deal with a person on an age-appropriate basis.
- Treat the person with dignity, respecting his or her space (and equipment).
- Admit it if you don't know how to help, followed by ". . . but I'd like to try."
- Avoid labeling a person by his or her disability; use "person with a disability" rather than "the disabled" or "the handicapped."
- Listen, even if it's difficult and tedious.
- Be persistent; sometimes their "no" means only "I don't want to bother you."
- Maintain a sense of humor.

—Conrad Mandsager

Tutoring and Educational Enrichment

After-school and evening tutoring programs are a low-cost, high-impact way to make a difference in the lives of young school students. Programs usually involve many of the church members. Since most churches have members that are already school teachers, these people can be encouraged to use their skills and talents to help organize and implement the tutoring program. This leads toward some excellent interaction and role-modeling for the youth.

Education Is Ministry

Fundamental to beginning an educational ministry is an understanding of its context within the church's broader mission. The concept of "Sunday school" was begun years ago to assist poor children in developing their reading and writing skills. Yet many churches have moved away from that wonderful ministry approach to viewing Sunday school as providing exclusively religious instruction. However, youth programs can be organized to meet both educational and spiritual needs.

One way to start a ministry is to follow this sequence:

- Explore the idea with the church as a whole, allowing broad input and capturing the interest of as many people as possible.
- Identify a coordinator who will carry the major leadership responsibility.
- Start a dialogue with the local schools, identifying ways the church can supplement their programs in students' lives.
- Plan a date to begin the program as soon as possible while also allowing time for adequate preparation and team building.
- Begin the program on a once-a-week schedule, meeting for approximately a half hour.

If the tutoring program becomes successful, the next step is to develop a learning center. This facility usually includes computers, textbooks, and desks—all similar to what might be found in a school classroom. Depending on the size of the program and financial resources, the center may be staffed either by volunteers or paid professionals. Many learning centers begin in Sunday school rooms before they move into new facilities used mainly for tutoring.

For further information on creative educational ministries from around the country, contact the Christian Community Development Association (3848 West Ogden Avenue, Chicago, IL 60623; phone 312/762-0994).

—*Wayne Gordon*

Job Training

Economic changes and problems produce a significant stream of newly unemployed persons to join the hard-core unemployed. Corporate downsizing, combined with a shrinking industrial factory base, has created an opportunity for congregations to help the unemployed. Churches can assist both their own members and those in the greater community by utilizing resources they might not know they possess.

A Vocational Second Chance

Job training does not necessarily require a vocational training school method of operation. Rather, an emphasis on developing interview skills, increasing literacy, gaining practical experience, and receiving technical assistance can offer people a second chance at a new or rejuvenated career. Here is one way to launch this ministry.

● *Set up a job-training committee.* The committee first decides which parts of the unemployed population in the community are in most need of help. Will it be unskilled workers, partially skilled workers, skilled workers, or management people? Once the target

groups are identified, the next step is to decide how large a program to undertake and what resources are available. Then the committee can decide if the project will use volunteers only or hire a full- or part-time director.

A volunteer appointed by the job-training committee could address inquiries from a "command central" either at the church or at a member's home, offering information about the job-training project. Many deacons and elders are leaders not only in their communities of faith but also in the business or academic worlds. Their advice and counsel within the committee can be invaluable.

● *Announce a regular schedule of daily activities.* Offer the ministry during normal business hours. This encourages people to function during the day just as they would if they were still employed, helping to avoid one of the first casualties of unemployment—damaged self-esteem. Establishing a team of volunteers who will be available during business hours and who can hold regular meetings with the unemployed to listen and offer emotional support is essential. Volunteers should also begin offering classes in job-search and interviewing skills.

If literacy skills are lacking, a cooperative venture with a local high school or junior college will produce outside volunteers who are happy to offer classes in a church basement. Should your church have access to an unused computer or two, classes in beginning word processing can be part of the program.

• *Offer unpaid work during training.* A church is a ready-made repository of practical job experiences. A part of the job-training project could include having participants work alongside church-maintenance people in repairing the roof or fixing an electrical problem. The custodian might teach someone how to use a floor buffer or clean kitchen facilities and equipment properly.

A cooking class that prepares food for church special events is another excellent practical job-training project. You might even find someone you or another church could hire full- or part-time.

• *Get church members networking.* Invite your members to post job openings from their employers on a special bulletin board, and ask representatives from various companies in your community to visit your job-training program to see it firsthand.

Naturally, it's wise to avoid promising anyone that you will find them a job. In the best of times, job hunting is difficult. Offering support is essential, but false promises only create false hope, more despair, and feelings of failure.

—Richard A. Roberts

Immigration and Refugee Work

In the parable of the Good Samaritan, Jesus calls us to demonstrate the power of the kingdom by crossing all social and cultural borders to assist a fellow traveler in need. This poignant parable forever redefines the concept of neighbor and directs us to act in the face of need. We must constantly ask ourselves, "Who is our neighbor?" The answer obviously includes immigrants and refugees.

A Welcome-Mat Ministry

All newcomers to the U.S. are *immigrants. Refugees* are those who have fled persecution and have been accepted by the American government for resettlement. Ministries to refugees and immigrants differ from other ministries in that they are designed to meet the unique needs of people who are new to the culture, the structure, the language, the customs of life in the United States.

How can your church get involved? Allow refugees and immigrants in the congregation to help define the opportunities. If the church is isolated from the immigrant community, contact immigrant churches or the county government to obtain demographics on the new arrivals in your community: How many immigrants arrived last year? Where did they come from? What languages do they speak? What agencies are working with refugees and immigrants? What services are missing? Then consider the forms of ministry your church might be able to offer in Christ's name.

Here are just some of many opportunities:

• *Resettle a refugee family.* There is a partnership between the U.S. government and the private sector that most Americans know little about. All U.S.-bound refugees arrive through U.S.-contracted agencies. There are five Christian agencies: the United States Catholic Conference, Lutheran Immigration and Refugee Services, Episcopal Migration Ministries, Church World Service of the National Council of Churches, and World Relief of the National Association of Evangelicals. These five agencies have a network of offices that cover almost every community in the United States.

A participating church assists in the care and maintenance of an arriving family for up to 90 days. This may include providing housing upon arrival, registering children for school, taking the family for medical checkups, stocking the refrigerator, collecting furniture, and—most important—making friends.

• *Maintain a clothes closet.* Refugees and other newly arrived immigrants may find themselves needing clothes for a new climate. A local church can collect, sort, repair, and maintain clothes for new arrivals. Coordination with the community will bring the church into the mainstream of service providers and will allow other agencies that work with immigrants to refer them to the church's clothing resources as well as to its other ministries.

• *Schedule ESL classes.* Immigrants need to learn English. Even those who find jobs upon arrival will need to acquire language skills to achieve advancement. Often, state funded ESL (English as a second language) programs offer classes during the day when many immigrants are working. An evening program for adults, with child care available, is a good ministry option for a church.

• *Start an after-school tutoring program.* Children of newly arrived immigrants often have difficulty doing schoolwork and homework because of language limitations and cultural differences. A church can coordinate with schools to provide after-school tutoring for immigrant children.

• *Create an employment network.* Immigrants need jobs, good employers, and benefits. Churches networking within communities can prepare job listings, teach newcomers how to complete applications, assist with transportation to and from interviews, and teach job-interview skills.

When churches stand shoulder-to-shoulder with new arrivals, the whole community will know that in Christ's kingdom the welcome mat is out.

—Peggy Gilbert

Respite Care and Hospice

Most pastors would give their right arms to have a person like Stephen in the local congregation. Stephen was Spirit filled, Scripture saturated, and steadfast unto death (Acts 6 and 7). But how did the apostles utilize this wonderfully gifted disciple? They appointed him to design the first outreach to home-bound widows in Jerusalem (Acts 6:1ff). The apostles must have sensed that half of the equation for "pure religion" meant taking care of those who could no longer take care of themselves (James 1:27).

If we hired Stephen to be a twentieth-century church consultant, this creative leader would likely draw our attention to the 30 million Americans who are 65 years of age and older. Most of them are healthy, living independently in their own homes. However, 20 percent do need some help with daily living, and 5 percent require the services of a hospital, hospice, or nursing home. What can we in the local church do to help?

Offer Respite Care

When a person needs help in daily living, a family volunteer usually offers some of the following "cups of cold water" in Jesus' name: *direct care*, including bathing, helping to the toilet, feeding, dressing, or walking; and *indirect care*, consisting of cooking, house cleaning, driving, banking, or dispensing medications.

But what happens when the family volunteer isn't available, undergoing surgery, for instance, or going on a business trip or caring for a sick child? Or what if the helper just needs a vacation? That's where respite care comes in. When the family caregiving gets temporarily interrupted, church-sponsored respite care can fill the gap.

During daytime hours, families can find respite from their caregiving duties through an adult day care center headquartered at the church. For longer periods of time, a family might engage a nursing home to secure a few days or weeks of respite care. The difference between family care and respite care is that the latter may cost money, occurs away from the family home, and provides a nurse on duty around the clock.

Though families must guard against "granny dumping," even the Good Samaritan paid the innkeeper two silver coins to provide substitute care during his absence (Luke 10:35). Joseph, too, had others helping keep the 17-year bedside vigil for his father, Jacob (Gen. 47:29; 48:1–2).

Support Hospice Ministries

When a person enters into the final stages of a terminal illness—and knows it—hospice can help. With its two trademark features, hospice helps people to: (1) remain as pain-free as possible, and (2) die at home, close to their family members. If we had entered a hospice during the Dark Ages, we would have been in an overnight resting place for weary travelers. Today, however, entering a hospice means

duced by the church, in particular the sale of indulgences that offered remission of sins for the buyer or whomever the buyer designated. The Reformers contended that the gospel offer of forgiveness was the unconditional gift of Christ and could not be sold by the church. The abuses of private confession also came under scrutiny. Appealing to the doctrine of the priesthood of all believers, Luther argued that anyone, not just a priest, could hear confession and pronounce God's forgiveness.

The Reformers devoted much attention to improving the quality of pastoral care and spiritual direction in the regions under their influence. Two important documents from this era are Zwingli's *The Shepherd* (1524) and Bucer's *On the True Care of Souls* (1538). Zwingli offered a biblical theology of the pastor and a thorough critique of the false prophets and shepherds occupying clerical offices. Beginning with Paul's "one another" statements, Bucer developed the concept of

---

for a weekend retreat. The first thing these pastors tell their lay officers is that by electing them to office, the congregation has asked them for spiritual leadership. Their brothers and sisters in the faith are counting on them for spiritual support and guidance. Parishioners need someone other than the pastor, someone who lives in the same 9-to-5 world they do, to show them that an authentic Christian life is really possible and that ordinary, everyday people can bear a powerful witness to Jesus Christ.

Credible Examples

A congregation rarely will exceed the spiritual reach and depth of its lay leaders. If lay leaders think Bible study is important, if they show up at advertised church events, if they exude an honest enthusiasm for ministry, service, and prayer, then (and only then) will the rest of the congregation begin to take lay leadership seriously. In short, if something is actually happening spiritually in the lives of lay leaders, their credibility as leaders will go through the roof.

So developing spiritual leadership among the members of our ruling boards begins with encouraging their individual growth in discipleship. We can provide Bible studies and yearly Bible-reading schedules. We can steer them toward books that will increase their theological understanding and sharpen their spiritual vision. We can take them with us on home and hospital visits and give them meaningful roles in worship services.

Why not encourage lay leaders to organize Bible studies or to say the grace at the next church potluck? While we ask for their best efforts, we need to leave room for imperfections. We let the congregation see we take lay leadership seriously by not trying to control everything ourselves. As leaders are allowed and encouraged to lead, they will.

—*Brent Mitchell*

mutual care (*aedification mutua*) in the local church.

Pastors in the Reformation era were encouraged to focus on preaching, teaching, visitation, and spiritual discipline. As Calvin put it: "The office of a true and faithful minister is not only publicly to teach the people over whom he is ordained pastor, but as far as may be, to admonish, exhort, rebuke and console each one in particular." In the Presbyterian Church of Scotland, Knox's *First Book of Discipline* delegated certain pastoral duties to elders, such as visitation, private counseling, and discipline.

Baxter's *Reformed Pastor* (1656) is the best known and most enduring statement of Puritan pastoral care. For Baxter, pastoral care consists of seven basic functions: converting the unconverted, giving advice to inquirers, building up the believers, shepherding the families in the parish, visiting the sick and dying, reproving the inpenitent, and exercising discipline. This approach to pastoral care was highly directive; that is, it depended upon the intervention and guidance of the pastor. The pastor was the expert on appropriate behavior as well as correct doctrine. Puritan pastoral care primarily addressed the individual's conscience and moral conduct. As a result of these features, the Puritan approach could fall into excessive casuistry and legalism.

As early as 1738, Wesley emphasized lay pastoral care in the Methodist class meetings and societies, in which Christians could confess their faults and temptations and receive encouragement and constructive criticism in return. These class meetings heralded the contemporary small-group and lay pastoral-care movements. In North America, the Methodist circuit rider and the Baptist lay preacher represented a new form of pastoral care on the frontier, where the parish-church system of Europe and the Atlantic seaboard was not yet established.

In the nineteenth century, revivalism and liberalism both made their marks on pastoral care. Frontier camp meetings and urban revivals focused the purpose of pastoral care on the process of conversion and the assurance of pardon. The holiness movement's emphasis on Christian perfection led to concern for eliminating "known sin" from one's life and attaining the "second blessing" of entire sanctification. Pentecostalism, an offshoot of the holiness movement, also sought a second blessing, which would be confirmed by speaking in tongues. Pentecostals also advocated the use of other supernatural gifts in pastoral care, such as healing and exorcism.

The rise of liberalism had a significant impact on the shaping of pastoral care in the nineteenth century. Reacting against the legalism of the Puritans and the perceived excesses of revivalism, liberalism encouraged a form of pastoral care suited to the temperament of the "modern era." Instruction in faith, for example, was no longer merely doctrinal instruction but an exploration in religious self-awareness. Discipline in the Reformation and Puritan sense virtually vanished in the mainline churches. As early as the 1840s, some Methodists were lamenting the disappearance of the class meetings. On the other hand, pastors spent more time visiting the sick and dying, and calling upon parishioners in their homes, offering personal encouragement and an inoffensive mixture of common-sense advice and religious insight.

Ahead of its time, Bushness's *Christian Nurture* (1847) suggested long-term Christian education beginning in childhood as preferable to leading adults into a crisis conversion experience. In a different vein, Rauschenbusch's *Pastoral Theology* (1908) offered a perspective on pastoral care fueled by the social gospel, which was born out of his ministry amid urban poverty and suffering.

• *Recent developments in pastoral care.* The twentieth century has witnessed several significant developments in pastoral care. First, an unmistakable feature of contemporary pastoral care has been the professionalization of ministry. Like other professionals, clergy have sought degrees and other credentials as benchmarks of competence in ministry. This trend has also led to the specialization of pastoral care. At the turn of the century, all pastors were generalists who could presumably do everything required of a church leader. Now many large churches have developed specialized care ministries staffed by specialists. Several pastoral theologians have warned of the "professional captivity of pastoral care," in which the biblical call for mutual edification gets replaced by the medical model of the therapist-patient relationship.

The discipline of psychology has made a significant impact on pastoral care in the twentieth century, from preparation for ministry to the methods of caregiving. In 1900, for example, students received little or no training in psychology. By the mid 1960s, however, clinical-pastoral education (CPE) and counseling were standard features of seminary education.

Another trend has been the proliferation of Christian counselors trained in graduate psychology programs. Some are affiliated with local churches, while many others are in private practice. Often thought of as pursuing a profession within a profession, Christian counselors frequently adopt techniques employed by their secular counterparts. Many larger congregations have established counseling centers, staffed by certified counselors and marriage and family therapists. Professionally led groups sponsored by local churches or by nationwide organizations have become an option for many unable to afford traditional psychotherapy. Smaller congregations have established referral networks with Christians working in secular, private, and public mental-health agencies.

A third trend, paradoxically, is the increasing role of the laity in providing pastoral care. Since the 1970s, lay-counseling training programs have equipped many lay men and women for primary pastoral care. Greeted initially with skepticism on the part of pastoral-care professionals, lay pastoral care continues to grow as believers discover their gifts and calling to ministry.

Small groups known as covenant groups or care groups are another type of lay pastoral care. The charismatic renewal movement lifts up prayer, the miraculous, and inner healing in pastoral care. In many churches prayer ministries serve as part of a comprehensive congregational-care strategy.

More recently, the Christian recovery movement has responded to the epidemic of abuse and addiction in North America society. Lay-led support groups utilize explicitly Christian versions of the now-famous Twelve-Step philosophy pioneered by Alcoholics Anonymous.

Transformation and Maturity

This survey of both the biblical and historical roots of pastoral care suggests a primary, two-fold purpose for Christian pastoral care, which is most explicitly conveyed in the New Testament writings: (1) transformation (*metanoia*) and (2) maturity (*teleis*). Transformation and maturity are both goals *and* processes, means *and* ends.

As a goal or end, transformation refers to a shift in one's fundamental life orientation toward Christ. *Metanoia* is a real change in a person's psychological and spiritual functioning brought about by the activity of God. Personal transformation is possible because of freedom in Christ, rather than because of a general human potential for change. Ray Anderson calls this the "therapeutic intervention of the grace of God" (Anderson 1990, 103–120). Christian pastoral care may thus affirm conversion as a turning toward Christ and an embracing of new life in his Spirit. It further aims to encourage and guide persons to and through this event.

As a process or means, *metanoia* indicates an ongoing evolution in which the person is always being transformed by the renewing of the mind (Rom. 12:2). Ongoing conversion is thus a process of reorientation to the source of wholeness, that is, to Christ himself. Like the event of conversion, the origin of the lifelong process of transformation is outside the self. Anderson comments: "Conversion as the saving work of the sanctifying Spirit of Jesus Christ is a work of grace which promotes mental health in healing the estranged and narcissistic individual" (Anderson 1990, 116). In view of this, pastoral care aims at sustaining and guiding others through an ongoing conversion, a life of personal transformation and change in the community of Christ.

embroiled churches in lengthy legal battles. Thus it is wise to avoid arbitrating in private disputes unless the procedures for doing so are clearly specified in the church's bylaws and all parties agree in writing to the ground rules.

In addition, when adults in church leadership are found to have abused children under their care, those in charge of discipline must take three immediate steps: (1) notify the police or other authorities, (2) remove the offender from any contact with children while the case is pending, and (3) write down the details of all discipline hearings from the beginning.

—*Michael E. Phillips*

17

Small Groups

The small-group movement has come of age. After fifty years of trial and error, the small group is now recognized as a primary vehicle for growing the church spiritually and numerically. However, the movement must be kept from veering off balance, as it can so easily do and has done sometimes in the past.

What can we do to keep from making the mistakes of the past? First, we need to understand the history of the small-group movement in order to recognize the roots of its contemporary strengths and weaknesses. Second, we can become familiar with the five basic types of groups and consider diligently how to encourage them within our congregations.

As people become available for small groups and willing to join one, they need to be offered a meaningful place to fit into Christ's body, a group within which they can "together with all the saints . . . grasp how wide and long and high and deep is the love of Christ" (Eph. 3:18).

How the Movement Began and Grew

The Mississippi—definitely a large river—is made up of many smaller streams. Likewise, the small-group movement today is a large movement composed of many small streams that have come together over the last fifty years.

- *1900–1950: Origins.* In general, we could say the movement started out in the student world as an attempt to get back to primitive Christianity. It was driven by a missionary passion to reach the world for Christ, and the strategy became the ever-multiplying "cell." North American tributaries included the Student Volunteer Movement, with Robert Speer and John Mott; the YMCA movement; and the spill-over from England of the Oxford Group and the Keswick "Deeper Life" movements. Biblical Seminary in New York (with its emphasis on inductive Bible study) and the experimental studies on group dynamics from Sara Little at Union Seminary were major influences.

- *1950–1960: The period of the prophets.* During this period, North America emerged from the Second World War as the major world power. Revival broke out at Wheaton, Asbury, Baylor, and other Christian schools. Campus Crusade for Christ and the Navigators went after the secular campuses. Billy Graham crusades led thousands to a personal faith in Christ and introduced them to ssmall groups for fellowship.

The small-group movement in the fifties was largely a parachurch movement. When a church did embrace small groups, the groups were an appendage to the program. Bible study was the focus, and the requirements for group membership eliminated all but the highly committed. It would be another thirty years before the church learned how to manage groups and provide a menu for all levels of commitment in the church.

Some of the most influential leaders during this period included: Sam Shoemaker (Faith at Work), Elton Trueblood (Yokefellows), Glenn Clark (Camps Furthest Out), Dawson Trotman (Navigators), C. Stacey Woods (InterVarsity), Bill Bright (Campus Crusade for Christ), E. Stanley Jones (Ashrams), and Frank Buchman (Moral Rearmament).

- *1960–1970: The movement takes off.* In this decade, the major denominations began to embrace small-groups as a technique for evangelism. They were heavily influenced by the Organizational Development movement. Some of the most influential seminaries turned to the American Psychological Association for group-therapy techniques and introduced CPE (clinical pastoral education) to seminary students.

Leaders during this period included Bruce Larson (Faith at Work), Samuel Emerick (Yokefellows), Ben Johnson (Institute of Church Renewal), and Don James (Pittsburgh Experiment). There were several church renewal "watering holes," where pastors went for training and personal renewal (Dayspring Retreat Center of the Church of the Saviour, Washington, D.C.; Laity Lodge in Leaky, Texas; Kirkridge in Bangor, Pennsylvania; and Yokefellow Institute at Earlham College in Richmond, Indiana).

The sixties were exciting years, but the influence of secular ideas may have set back the explicitly Christian small-group movement. The therapy model of closed groups (for reasons of confidentiality) crippled the cell-multiplication system. Also, the social-action focus in the mainline denominations tended to go overboard. Elizabeth O'Connor warned in her book *Journey Inward, Journey Outward* that "any group that neglects the journey inward for the journey outward will burn out." By the end of the sixties, the small-group movement had burned out. It would be another twenty years before the movement's leaders learned to keep the balance.

• *1970–1980: The period of excess.* Political idealism was shattered by the war in Vietnam, and the church was burned out on social action. A new crop of leaders emerged that were more attuned to personal growth, such as Carl Rogers (Human Potential), Fritz Pearls (National Training Labs), and Ira Progoff (Journaling Workshops). Some of the retreat centers and leadership-training ministries moved away from Christ-centered small groups to form human-encounter small groups.

So after going overboard on Bible study in the fifties and social action in the sixties, the small-group movement went overboard on personal growth in the seventies. Books demonstrating this trend included Thomas Harris's *I'm OK, You're OK*, Sam Keen's *To a Dancing God*, Ira Progoff's *At a Journal Workshop*, Charles Schultz's *Joy*, and Scott Peck's *The Road Less Traveled*. These were primarily secular books, but they reflected the spirit of this decade, when the small-group movement turned to personal introspection and human interaction. Often psychological tests were promoted as kick-off materials for starting groups. The church on the whole followed the humanistic education model for personal growth in small groups. It would be another ten years before the small-group movement learned how to keep a healthy balance between psychology and theology.

• *1980–1990: The integration period.* Church growth studies demonstrated that the fastest growing churches in the world (particularly in Third-world countries) were cell churches. Church-planting agencies adopted small-group techniques, and the church turned to church growth technology. Leaders in this movement were Donald McGavran, Peter Wagner, and Eddie Gibbs (Fuller Theological Seminary); Carl George (Charles E. Fuller Institute of Church Growth); and Win Arn (Institute for American Church Growth). The influence of David (formerly Paul) Yonggi Cho in Korea was also significant.

Tough times in the eighties caused the church to deal with the survival instincts of people. This has brought about a greater balance of the three basic needs of any Christian small group: Bible study, caring, and multiplication. By the end of the eighties, a number of churches had demonstrated a workable model for "growing the

To recruit the right people, leaders first begin to publicly emphasize the importance of caring, while stressing that counseling is a gift that many believers may not possess, that a rigorous training program is required before the potential lay counselor will become active in the counseling ministry, and that completion of the program will not necessarily make one a qualified lay counselor. This helps discourage causal involvement in the program.

Second, it should be announced that there will be a selection procedure to enter the program. This may cause some resistance and criticism, but it helps prevent insensitive, immature, and otherwise unsuitable people from entering the program. If leaders are careful not to put down anyone, most people will see the value in some initial screening.

Supervisors work at maintaining oversight by constantly defining and restating the goals of each case. They scrutinize the methods used and discuss any evident biases of the lay counselor. They also give valuable encouragement, pointing out positive aspects of the counselor's work, providing opportunities for academic study, and directing counselors toward specialized training experiences.

Occasionally a supervisor will be faced with the need to discipline a lay counselor for failure to carry out commitments or for unethical conduct. Discipline should be handled simply and directly by clearly explaining the reasons for concern and pointing out the consequences.

Selecting Lay Counselors

Volunteer lay counselors want to utilize their gifts to help others, but such laudable desires do not automatically qualify someone for lay counseling. Some people may volunteer to gain status, control others, or avoid their own emotional problems.

The supervisor, in selecting lay counselors, should look for key indications of fitness, such as:

• *Formal preparation for the task.* Lay counselors should be trained in the overall counseling process as well as in the specifics of the cases they will likely handle (such as premarital counseling, marital support, parenting, etc.).

• *Self-awareness.* Potential lay counselors must be aware of their own deeper motivations and feelings—and be willing to honestly express these to the supervisor. It's great if the potential counselor has already progressed through his or her own psychotherapy.

• *Personal maturity.* Lay counselors should show emotional and spiritual maturity, as indicated by the supervisor's interactions with them and by the reports of their personal references.

• *Communication skills.* Lay counselors must have the ability to listen with great concentration and empathy, and then communicate clearly and directly.

—*Randy Christian*

Criticism will be reduced (and some personal needs will be met) if the church conducts a prior class on the ministry of caring and the discovery of spiritual gifts. This class could be open to everyone, followed by a more in-depth class open only to those who successfully complete the selection screening.

Screening might involve:

• A brief written statement acknowledging the applicant's adherence to the church's doctrinal positions, plus a testimony of personal Christian experience and the applicant's reasons for wanting to be in a lay counseling program.

• A letter of recommendation from two or three people who know the applicant well.

• An interview during which the class leader and another church leader begin to assess the spiritual maturity, stability, and motivation of the applicant.

• A psychological test or two. Many churches use the Taylor/Johnson Temperament Analysis, although research has demonstrated that a test known as the 16PF is the best predictor of counseling effectiveness. Such tests have to be obtained and interpreted by a trained psychologist or other certified person.

How Are Lay Counselors Trained?

Several programs have been developed for counselor training. Obviously, any training program will be more effective when the teacher has some familiarity with professional counseling techniques and counselor training, although such background information is not absolutely necessary. Typically, training will proceed in three phases: pretraining, training, and posttraining.

• *The pretraining phase* involves selection of materials, announcement of the program, and selection of the participants. If a church decides to do an initial course on caring and the discovery of spiritual gifts, it might want to discuss such books as my *The Joy of Caring*, Ray Stedman's *Body Life*, or Rick Yohn's *Discover Your Spiritual Gift and Use It*.

• *The training phase* should give students opportunities to learn by listening to lectures, reading, observing, and gaining personal experience. Most programs involve at least 40 to 50 hours of training (some of which may be completed at home), spread over a period of several months. It is best to keep the training groups small (12 to 15), to meet regularly, and to use at least some printed materials.

The training sessions should allow time for students to share about themselves and to express their own needs and insecurities as they discuss complex problems such as depression or homosexuality. The sessions should make use of student role plays—brief periods of prac-

Like prayer, however, Scripture can be misused in counseling, and with greater harm. We can use the Bible in a way that short-circuits the counseling process. The counselee describes a few symptoms of her problem, and immediately verses begin popping into our minds. Before she can finish her story, we want to interrupt with last month's sermon on "How to Mend Your Marriage."

If we become trigger happy with Scripture, we will fail to hear counselees' true concerns. As a result we won't understand their problems' contexts and causes, and worse, we won't grasp how *they* understand the Bible. We can't hit the target unless we know what the target is. If we go too quickly to "thus saith the Lord" before we know what saith the counselee, we won't see what the real issues are. Thus, we need to be patient in drawing people out. That said, here are ways to employ the Bible in counseling:

Unless a pastor is trained in psychopathology, the most responsible action is referral to a trusted psychologist or psychiatrist for diagnosis. While treatment is under way, we may want to counsel the person in the steps of Christian commitment, encouraging a surrender to the claims of Christ. It is possible, however, that the professional treatment temporarily may need to take precedence over spiritual guidance, simply because the disease needs to be under control before the person can comprehend spiritual matters adequately.

• *Investigate the need for regeneration.* One of the great drawbacks of secular counseling or psychotherapy is that it may not deal directly with the core problem of human existence: our alienation from God. As Christian counselors we can prepare a person to be receptive to God's work. We can help remove the obstacles of childhood traumas or distorted God images so that God's grace can become effective.

Even explicitly Christian counseling does not do the work of grace; it merely aids it. It is nothing more than burden bearing as we are instructed by Bible passages such as Galatians 6:2. We are helping others rely upon the greatest burden bearer of all (see Matt. 8:17).

• *Consider supernatural causes.* At what point should one consider the possibility of supernatural or demonic causes for a problem and invoke deliverance as the remedy? Only when the more obvious causes have been eliminated.

If there is a history of severe depression in the immediate family of a troubled person, for instance, psychiatric treatment must be given first consideration. It is gross negligence to move beyond this diagnosis without thoroughly exploring whether the symptoms have physical causes.

Another word of caution: We should never try to diagnose supernatural causes by ourselves, but rather seek corroboration from others and hold ourselves accountable to the corporate discernment.

—Archibald D. Hart

• *Use Scripture not to condemn but to outline a new direction.* This is how Jesus used the Word as he ministered to those who were sincere. Christ's use of Scripture differed radically from the Pharisees'; they used Scripture to condemn people. They focused on the past—the sins already committed—and how God's commandments condemn such conduct.

Christ focused on the present and the future, on how a person can restore a relationship with God and how to maintain that relationship. With the woman caught in adultery, he refused to condemn but rather said, "Go your way and sin no more." Most people know when

---

Schizophrenia or Demon Possession?

Scores of emotionally troubled people every year are told they have an "evil spirit" possessing them, but demon possession is rarely the problem. The hopelessness such a false label engenders in the sufferer (especially after exorcisms fail to cure the problem) can often do more harm than the original problem.

Pastoral counselors need to be able to distinguish between demonic possession and serious mental disorders, such as schizophrenia. The first task is to make certain that no psychiatric or organic cause is being overlooked. Only after all possible natural explanations are exhausted should we consider investigating demonic possession.

Recognizing Schizophrenia

Schizophrenia is a physical disease. Because its sufferers exhibit such bizarre symptoms, it is sometimes labeled as demon possession. But just as we learned with epilepsy (another disease formerly labeled as demon possession), we now know that schizophrenia is the result of a defect in brain chemistry.

Often medication can be the cure. Any delay in starting the right medication for treating schizophrenia can impact the sufferer's long-term recovery. So misdiagnosis here can have serious consequences. This is especially true for a form of schizophrenia that sometimes starts in late adolescence.

Some basic symptoms of schizophrenia include: extreme forms of social isolation or withdrawal; marked inability to function as wage earner, student, or homemaker; markedly peculiar behavior (collecting garbage, talking to self in public, hoarding food); extreme loss of attention to personal hygiene and grooming; digressive, vague, over-elaborate conversation, or lack of conversation, or lack of content in conversation; odd beliefs or magical thinking that affect the person's behavior (being superstitious, believing in clairvoyance, telepathy, or the idea that "others can feel my feelings"); unusual experiences (recurrent illusions, sensing the presence of a force or person not actually present); and marked lack of initiative or energy.

they are breaking God's plan. The resulting destruction eventually forces them to face the need for change.

Jesus was also sensitive to each individual. He understood people intimately and used Scripture in accordance with that insight. He helped people understand their motives and attitudes. Then he offered forgiveness, a fresh start, and a new discipline.

• *Back into Scripture.* People understand most terms, including biblical terms, based on their experience. Until we understand their reference points—their contexts and definitions—we easily miss the mark with Scripture. In fact, most of the time when we start handing

---

What might appear to be demon possession, then, usually will be some form of schizophrenia. This is important because falsely attributing emotional problems to demons has several dangers: It keeps the sufferer from recognizing and confessing *human* sinfulness, it emphasizes Satan's power inappropriately, and, most important, it delays the introduction of effective treatment.

Schizophrenia is a complex disease. If a pastor suspects it in a counselee, he or she should make the appropriate referral immediately. Delaying treatment for a problem like schizophrenia can significantly decrease the likelihood of the sufferer's return to normality.

Diagnosing Possession

If this is schizophrenia, though, what does demon possession look like? The characteristics of demon possession are not easy to discern. However, those who have extensive experience with possession look for such factors as:

• *A striking lack of human warmth.* The possessed seem barren and empty, and they lack empathy.

• *The presentation of a new personality.* The person's voice and ex- pressions change, and he or she begins acting and speaking like a different person. (However, this is also seen in "multiple personality disorders," a severe psychological problem associated with childhood abuse.)

• *Marked revulsion to Christian symbols.* The cross, the Bible, and other Christian symbols often make the possessed extremely uncomfortable. (However, schizophrenics may also display this reaction.)

• *Strange physical phenomena.* Many observers describe an inexplicable stench, freezing temperatures, flying objects, and a "smooth, stretched skin" (see Malachi Martin's *Hostage to the Devil*).

• *Supernatural behavioral transformations.* For example, the victim may display "possessed gravity" — in other words, he or she cannot be moved physically, or can levitate.

Obviously, then, possession is not as common as might be supposed, and many so-called possessions have more natural explanations. Diagnosis of demon possession is a matter of eliminating all possible mental disorders as causes of bizarre presenting problems before proceeding to supernatural explanations.

—Archibald D. Hart

out biblical injunctions to "love" or "submit to one another" or "serve one another" without probing how they understand these biblical ideas, counselees end up feeling frustrated and condemned.

For example, several years ago a husband and wife came for counseling. The wife's biggest complaint was "My husband isn't romantic enough."

What he heard her saying, though, was "He's not good enough in bed." With such a narrow perspective on the term *romantic*, he was devastated, because he had been raised to take great pride in his ability to perform sexually.

I explored her complaint and discovered she was really saying, "He isn't attentive to me during the day."

In a similar way, after we discover what the counselee means by certain biblical phrases, we can explain what the phrase means in its context, using their understanding by way of contrast. Then we can help people discover the truth of Scripture for themselves by assigning homework, such as having them fill out worksheets on abuse, alcohol, or marriage and family.

Use Small Groups Strategically

A pastoral counselor can employ the home-field advantage: the church community. Pastors lead a group of people with the potential to serve and to love others into well-being. But since such groups can easily turn into quagmires of dysfunction, we need to lead the groups in strategic ways.

● *Supervise involvement.* We dare not just send people to support groups or ask them to get involved in Bible studies without watching over them as they get involved. Some people even need to be discouraged altogether from small groups, at least until they can participate in them maturely.

Some people hug their hurts. They try to wrest significance by drawing attention to their problems. In a small group, these people will inevitably plunder everyone's attention and energies, making their needs the centerpiece.

For example, one young woman I counseled came from a severely dysfunctional home. To get the attention she craved, she created crises, and these were the only times her parents would notice her. She developed a drinking problem and then a pattern of dating men who exploited her. She brought the same pattern into church. Every group she was in sooner or later had to turn its full energies toward her. She liked that; she didn't really want her problems solved.

We can try to help such a person understand the patterns she has gotten stuck in and teach her new behaviors. But it will be slow going, and it demands careful direction.

● *Help spawn small groups.* The key to small groups is intentionality. We need to know exactly what we want to accomplish and then make sure the people know what the group is trying to do in relation to the broad ministry of the church.

In the church I serve, our primary small-group format is what we call "Circles of Concern." For a month, on Tuesday evenings, we gather a group to discuss a particular problem, with the goals of: (1) providing useful information about the problem, and (2) encouraging interaction among those facing the common difficulty.

We designed one Circle of Concern for people making decisions about what to do with elderly parents. At the first meeting a geriatric worker talked to the group. The second week a nursing home supervisor discussed the legal and financial factors involved in placing a loved one into such care. The third week I taught a Bible study on how God perceives the aging process and our need to be sensitive toward the elderly. The final Tuesday, a panel of those who had made these decisions told their experiences and the lessons learned.

Other topics that lend themselves to this type of small group include life as a single, parenting children who grew up in church but are no longer walking with Christ, financial planning, retirement, long-term illness, specific emotions such as anger, and marriage enrichment (one for those married up to five years, another for those married five to fifteen years, another for those fifteen years and more).

Encourage Worship Attendance

Because people in crisis need all the spiritual input possible, many pastors insist that their counselees attend worship. The heart and mind can be healed in public worship in ways that cannot happen in the counseling office. In worship, desperate and lonely people can sense the presence and power of God. Such sunshine through the window proves especially vital for those who feel distant from God, separated from him by their problems. No matter what their counseling issues, people do need the support of the church body and the inspiration and renewal of church worship to stabilize them.

Counselees often need a nudge to get to church, however. A simple "I'll be looking for you on Sunday" helps. Sometimes we can introduce them to someone who has weathered similar troubles. Attending church with a friend like that can reverse the feeling that the church is threatening by making it invitingly familiar. To ease the transition into the relationship, pastor, counselee, and "sponsor" may want to sit down together to begin to build the church network for the counselee.

A counselee's involvement in church does present two hurdles. After a couple of sessions, we may want to tell a counselee, "A time will come fairly soon when you'll be sitting in the congregation on Sunday morning and you'll think, *He's preaching at me,* or *He's letting these people know about my problem.* But that won't be the case at all. In the normal course of preaching through Scripture, I unavoidably deal with problems many people in the congregation have. Be assured I won't put you at risk, and if you think I am, come and talk to me."

We may also need to tell counselees, "Then the time will come when you're past the crisis, and you'll think, *That man in the pulpit knows more personal things about me than anyone else in the world,* and you'll be uncomfortable with that. You'll feel like packing your bags, moving elsewhere, and starting over. But you need to resist that feeling. What I know about you should be the basis for trust and a strong relationship, not for running away." We must keep on guard for signs of detachment. When counselees pull away, we need to contact them immediately to begin to pull them back in.

Spiritual resources for counseling, though not automatically effective, are supernaturally effective. When used with wisdom, they pierce the very core of a person's being, as Scripture says, "penetrating even to dividing soul and spirit, joints and marrow," healing where other methods cannot touch. I would not want to counsel anyone without them.

—*Gary Gulbranson*

Resources
Bridges, J. 1978. The pursuit of holiness. Colorado Springs: NavPress.
Colson, C. 1992. The body. Dallas: Word.
Morling, G. 1987. The quest for serenity. Waco: Word.
Whitney, D. 1991. Spiritual disciplines of the Christian life. Colorado Springs: NavPress.
Wright, H. 1986. Self-talk, imagery, and prayer in counseling. Waco: Word.

Premarital Counseling

In the exciting time before the marriage ceremony, couples are open to building the best marriage they can; our aim is to coach them toward that goal. The following steps can help these sessions run smoothly while addressing the important issues.

• *Establish a relationship.* Begin by building a friendship with the couple through positive, easy questions: How did you meet? How did you decide this is the one you want to marry?

After establishing rapport, follow with questions such as: Which of you felt the most discomfort in coming to see me, and why? How do you feel when visiting each other's families?

• *Cover counseling expectations.* Couples respond well when given three or four topics to choose from. A list of options might include misconceptions of love and marriage, ways to increase friendship, practical issues in marriage, romantic love, and Christian marriage.

• *Uncover misconceptions about marriage.* One way to stimulate discussion in this area is to give a "test," asking the couple to mark as true or false a list of statements, such as "Getting angry is better than being critical" or "Loneliness will be cured by marriage."

Amazing things happen. Couples laugh. They disagree openly. They get nervous. They show frustration. They reveal expectations.

Getting Practical

The bulk of the sessions should cover such practical issues as:

• *Affection and sexuality.* We can ask: Where do you find information on sexuality? What is sexual love? What will you do if one of you is more highly sexed than the other?

Potential areas of tension include a partner's right to know about the other's sexual past, traumatic experiences such as rape or incest, and role expectations, including feelings about headship and submissiveness. We must be pointedly practical on these issues.

• *Values.* Issues here include occupations, whether and when to have children, and family life. A helpful exercise is to have them write their values on colored cards, using the red cards for nonnegotiable values, yellow for important but modifiable ones, and green for flexible ones.

• *Religious faith.* Couples should share their faith experiences while being made aware of how different religious journeys develop and sometimes clash. We must press for concreteness: How often do you expect to go to church? What happened the last time your fiancée asked you for forgiveness?

• *Communication.* To encourage this, we can suggest the couple promise to meet weekly to compare calenders and ask about the other's emotional well-being. Some couples commit to two mini-honeymoons yearly after their marriage, even if only overnights.

• *Nurture.* We tend to nurture a spouse in the way *we* want to be nurtured. If the wife is nurtured by exercise, she may buy a jogging suit for her spouse, who hates athletics but loves a night at home reading. The aim is for couples to respect each other's nurture needs, even if they don't understand them.

• *Christian marriage.* Psychologists say every marriage has a *contract*, perhaps implied if not written or discussed, and usually the parties perceive the contract differently. More fundamental, however, is the sacred bond of *covenant* that transcends the legal ties, and so we discuss at length what God means to their union.

• *Ceremony procedures.* We can present copies of different vows—from high church to contemporary—for the couple to consider, and then review the meaning behind the Scripture readings, prayers, and questions of intent. Then we can sit back and watch them pore over the details of the service, observing how they make decisions.

—Bruce Rowlison

Guidelines

Here are three general guide-lines that can help balance em-pathy and objectivity:

• *Listen ready to believe.* Child sexual-abuse victims disclose their painful story to an average of nine people before anyone believes them. They're usually told by the abuser that no one will believe their story. Unfortunately, it is often true that the victim's only escape from one adult's transgression is the righteous indignation of another adult.

Most children assume pastors are interested in truth, so many victims open up to them, even after refusing to give details to others.

Statistics tell us that only one in a thousand disclosures proves false, and most of these are misunder-stood statements made to parents who turn frantic. The rest are usual-ly from adolescent girls afraid they may have become pregnant by a boyfriend. False claims typically prove easy to check; the story changes as it is retold.

• *Blow the whistle wisely.* In nearly every state, pastors suspecting child abuse are *required* to notify authori-ties. But family members need to be told as well. Eighty percent of all sexual abuse occurs within the fam-ily. Fathers and step-fathers are the largest offender group. Then come other male relatives, then mothers, then baby-sitters. Only 9 percent of abusers are unknown to their victims.

Therefore, we frequently have the responsibility of informing a nonoffending parent about the de-tails of the spouse's abuse. The best way is the direct way: "Your child found it too difficult to talk with you about this subject, so I'm com-pelled to tell you myself. Susie is being sexually abused by your husband."

This head-on approach has two advantages. First, the shock value definitely gets the parent's atten-tion. Second, if we begin to waffle and say, "Well, we're not really sure if it's true, but we think maybe there could be something possibly wrong . . ." the parent will rarely act on what we report. Coming across as unsure, we give the parent license to act as if nothing is hap-pening, and that's counterproduc-tive. Directness imparts a sense of certainty and urgency.

• *Keep the proper distance.* We should steer away from making long-term promises to the victim of sexual abuse. The victim needs to understand our role as counselors and that we cannot be on twenty-four-hour call.

This rule is as much for the vic-tim's good as it is for our own san-ity. Sexual-abuse victims often feel the need to cling to those who show love and affection. To compensate for the lack in the past, they often will demand too much from the counselor.

For example, one young victim of abuse phoned me an average of three to four times a day. At least once a day, she would ask me to come over to counsel her. She fre-quently hinted at suicide, as if my refusal would set off a regrettable but inevitable chain of events. I fi-nally had to tell her, "You just can't keep calling me like this. Let me tell you the reasons for your calls as I see them." I went on to tell her my understanding of *why* she was call-ing: her strong need for affirmation, her dependency, her fear of being rejected.

Support groups for victims and families, when guided by a sympathetic pastor or lay leader, can become a unique forum for significant sharing and prayer. They both help the victims and remove some of the need for excessive clinging to the counselor.

—*Michael E. Phillips*

Counseling Abusers

It's hard to counsel people who we may consider unlikable or who deeply repel us because of their shocking actions. Christian counselors frequently struggle with this problem when working with sexual and physical abusers, even though they know that *every* form of sin is offensive to God. Counselors who feel unable to put their feelings of disgust or contempt aside should be honest about this fact and be prepared to make a referral.

When we do take on abuse cases, we need to remind ourselves that abusers are not all alike. There is a significant difference, for example, between "normal" and "abnormal" abuse. Normal abuse is the kind most people *could* be tempted to commit, such as striking a spouse in the heat of an argument. This type of abuse is by far the most common, and the abuser is often able to change the behavior with adequate counseling.

Abnormal abuse, on the other hand, is the kind that most people would *not* be tempted to commit under any circumstance, such as sexually molesting a child. While it gets much publicity, abnormal abuse is much less common than the other type, and the prognosis for the abuser is not encouraging.

The process of counseling the abuser should focus on two pur-suits: to monitor the client to reduce the risk of further offense, and to address the root problems—the deeper psychological, relational, or systemic reasons the abuse occurs.

Monitoring the Client

Regardless of people's stated intention to change, they should not be placed in a position to abuse again until they are making significant progress on the root problems. The question "Can he be trusted?" is best answered by "He can be trusted to be exactly who he is." Even though he or she may have legitimately sought and received forgiveness, the psychological sources of the abuse no doubt remain. In other words, forgiveness does not insure that sinful behavior will not repeat itself. While some Christians may feel this is unduly judgmental, the counselor has a duty to help abusers by assisting them in avoiding the temptation to sin.

We can monitor clients at two levels. At the first level, we provide accountability partners who maintain contact with the abuser whenever he or she might have access to a potential victim. This type of monitoring also provides schedules and structures to help the client avoid tempting situations altogether. The second level is involuntary monitoring or legal constraint, such as putting into effect court restraining orders, electronic monitoring, or institutionalization.

Addressing the Root Problems

Physical and sexual abuse often flow from the abuser's own history of being an abused child. In such situations, the abuser will not change without fully exploring the deep woundedness of the past. When the counselor is not able to work with these foundational issues on a long-term basis, the abuse is likely to happen again and again.

While a pastor may continue to work with an abuser in a specific role, abusers should be referred to trained counselors who specialize in working with such cases when: (1) the abuse fits the "abnormal" description, (2) the abuser has a history of previous abuse, (3) the abuser is unrepentant or justifies the behavior, (4) the abuser is not making progress dealing with root problems.

In counseling abusers, we must not forget that our first responsibility is to those who cannot protect themselves—the victims. Even if the abuser does not respond to counseling, he or she can be monitored to prevent an opportunity to abuse again.

—Randy Christian

Job and Vocational Counseling

Pastors often serve on the front lines of job and vocational counseling. Young people come to us searching for ways to invest their lives in the world of work. Adults come, seeking guidance for potential career changes. Retired people find their way to our doors, looking for new challenges. Pink-slip victims seek us out, too — confused, angry, and disheartened — needing support and direction.

Counseling Guidelines

Here are some general guidelines for conducting counseling sessions with all kinds of job seekers.

• *Concentrate on passion more than perks.* God created people with a variety of interests. One person's passion is another's prison, and no matter how many perks come with a job, if a person doesn't enjoy it, he or she will find it hard to continue for long. While every job has its tedious or disappointing aspects, when we're in the right vocation, our passion usually outweighs the pain. As counselors, we can help people explore and identify the kinds of activities that genuinely interest and motivate them — a productive first step.

• *Look for intrinsic value in the vocation.* Our level of commitment to a career is directly related to our perception of how much we are needed. Pastors can help by encouraging job seekers to identify the intrinsic value of a potential vocation. If people know that others really do need them and what they provide through their work, they will enjoy their work more, even if it is difficult. If, however, people feel that they and what they do are unimportant to others, then no matter how well they are paid, they will find little joy in their work.

• *Have people count the cost of becoming competent.* Just being interested in a vocation isn't enough. Louis Pasteur once said, "In the field of observation, chance favors only the prepared minds." The same principle holds true in vocational searches: opportunity favors the prepared. Competence is essential in our competitive age, and the prerequisite to competence is the discipline to prepare.

The dictionary defines *vocation* not only as a "divine call to . . . a career or occupation" but also as a "sense of fitness for a career or occupation." We can help people test the reality of their desires by asking them to consider: *Am I really prepared to become a disciple of this vocation?* And we will want to be ready with suggestions about where to get good training if the client answers in the affirmative.

• *Minister to emotional needs after a job loss.* When people lose their jobs, they experience *grief* over the loss of meaningful activities, colleagues, self-esteem, confidence, and self-reliance; *anger* at being terminated; *fear* about financial needs; and *depression* (anger turned inward), accompanied by a sense of helplessness and hopelessness. The counselor must work at two levels in such cases, providing both a listening ear during a time of great stress and offering practical resources for finding training and new employment opportunities.

• *Confirm the call through the church.* The church ought to confirm a Christian's vocational calling. When we find our calling, we sense our lives are fitting into a field of work consistent with who God has made us to be. Our inner awareness, however, can be confirmed, expanded, or corrected by others because God's call has both personal and corporate dimensions. Since vocation grows from the awareness that God uses people to meet the needs of others, the church can help awaken people to their true callings.

—Michael Jinkins

Counseling Cult Members

"My daughter has joined a religious cult. What can I do?" Sometime in ministry it's likely a parent will say this to us. It is a moment of enormous emotional and spiritual importance. Our response will depend on the answers we give to five key questions.

Short-term Questions

• *Is the cult dangerous?* The first thing to determine is whether or not the young person is in any physical or psychological danger. Determine the degree of danger by finding out as much as possible

ry five preschoolers, every six first and second graders, every seven third and fourth graders, every eight fifth and sixth graders, every ten junior highs, and every dozen teens.

The team should divide tasks so that no one person is overwhelmed. For example, recruit teachers' aides to assist with memory work, attendance taking, and other routine tasks, and recruit craft leaders and aides to handle that part. Plenty of support workers are needed—secretaries, kitchen workers, recreation leaders, supply clerks, and worship leaders. The more people involved in vbs, the greater the enthusiasm for it. The more people involved, the less the likelihood of worker burnout.

It takes plenty of work to recruit a staff. Likely recruits include Sunday school teachers, youth coaches, public school teachers who may not teach Sunday school regularly, newcomers to the congregation who may not yet have found a place of ministry, college students home for the summer, and high school students to assist an experienced teacher. And these workers need the necessary know-how and materials to do the job.

One idea that works well is to have a vbs director-in-training working alongside the current director, with the understanding that the person in training will lead the effort the following year. This arrangement assures continuity and creativity—and saves considerable supervisory time.

Curriculum and Followup

The choice of curriculum is critical. Most leadership teams prefer to select a published resource, while a few teams choose to develop their own materials. The wide array of colorful visuals, teacher's and pupil's books, songbooks, and environmental helps is the strong lure of commercial curriculum. The opportunity to meet specific needs is the appeal of developing curriculum locally. Whatever curriculum is chosen should be Bible-based, need-related, educationally sound, attractive, and easy to use, even by relatively untrained teachers.

Followup assures success. The planning team should have a strategy for contacting newcomers. They should decide how to express appreciation to workers and how to integrate them into other places of ministry within the church program. They may want to plan follow-up activities (day camps, Bible clubs, youth groups, etc.) to maintain contact with new participants as well to provide further ministry to children within the congregation.

—*Eleanor Daniel*

Children's Ministries

Children's ministry is a relative newcomer to the church vocabulary. Though churches have carried out ministry to children for years through programs such as Vacation Bible Schools, it is still in many ways an emerging field that calls for creative planning and programming.

A Total Church Effort

What do we mean by children's ministry? It is a total church effort to meet the needs of children, from birth through elementary school. Naturally, it includes Sunday school, children's church, vacation Bible school, Bible clubs—all covered elsewhere in this book. But it may also include camps, tutoring, after-school activities, choirs, support groups for children with special needs or problems, special summer activities, latchkey day-care programs, and services for parents.

The objectives of children's ministry should be consistent with the objectives of the church. It should seek to meet the identified needs of children within the congregation and in the community. It should also reach out to find children—and their families—and attract them to the church. A third objective would be to minister to the children's families.

Planning children's ministry can be the function of a ministry team charged with the responsibility. The team may be a subgroup of the Christian education ministry team or it may be organized by the pastor or the general church leadership. The children's ministry team can evaluate existing programs (the scope defined by their supervisors), identify areas of need, prioritize the needs, and launch the programs chosen.

The team needs to exercise two cautions: Not to try to do more than the money and people resources will allow, and not to program so much that the ministry infringes on family time. It is far better to confine efforts to two or three special programs, doing them with excellence.

Many Avenues of Approach

Churches have found diverse ways to carry out good children's ministry. Some churches have developed outstanding latchkey programs that meet the needs of elementary children after school. These programs often provide tutoring, supervised study times, recreation opportunities, and spiritual teaching. Other churches offer a day-care program for the community and then follow it up with ongoing ministry to parents in order to integrate them into the total ministry of the church.

Summer is a special time to plan children's activities. Some churches make sure that children from both inside and outside the church go to camp, even if that means providing camp scholarships. Some churches have planned day-camp programs. Many have a special activity day per week in which children are involved in fun and educational activities.

Providing support groups for children is a growing area of ministry opportunity. Children who have experienced divorce often need special help. Children dealing with grief (the loss of a parent or grandparents, especially) can benefit from a support group. The same is true for children with special physical, intellectual, emotional, or social problems. The parents of these children have similar needs and would profit from ministry that parallels the support they themselves may be receiving. Many congregations already have a cadre of professionals who can use their skills in support-group settings.

Effective children's ministry requires spiritually mature, compassionate, stable adults to lead it. Many adults with these basic qualities can be taught the leadership, teaching, and listening skills necessary for the specific ministry. College interns may well make a valuable contribution, but they rarely carry out good children's ministry without the continuing involvement of more mature adults.

The future of children's ministry is limited only by our imaginations. Plenty of needs permeate our communities and churches, and we can find the needs and meet them.

—*Eleanor Daniel*

Christian Clubs

Club programs for children and youth have served North American churches for more than a century. Many continue to function as parachurch agencies, though denominations and local congregations have often absorbed them or created their own club programs. Historically, the club phenomenon can be traced to the Sunday school and nineteenth-century youth organizations such as the Society of Christian Endeavor and the YMCA, begun by Christians eager to evangelize and disciple young people whom they believed churches were neglecting. Today, most clubs are sponsored by churches.

Club Characteristics

Christian clubs perform various functions, including: evangelizing youth, teaching and applying biblical principles to life, supplementing Sunday school while providing physical activity and social development for the church's youth, providing a Christ-centered alternative to secular youth organizations, and fostering healthy adult-child relationships, often to compensate for family failures. Churches investigating sponsorship of a club should examine their own goals and determine which club programs are a suitable fit.

Almost all Christian clubs offer a similar set of program elements, with the curriculum emphasizing Scripture memorization, Bible stories, and discussion. Most clubs include games and craft projects in their meetings, while many add personal-achievement activities (outlined in handbooks) with appropriate awards and recognition. Invariably, club meetings conclude with devotions or personal testimonies. Camping, service projects, and competitive sports lend the extracurricular dimension to regular club meetings.

Churches typically consider clubs a part of the Christian education program, to be supervised by a Christian education director or committee. Since the clubs are often more successful than the Sunday school in attracting unchurched youth, a club should be treated as an outreach arm of the church, as well. These clubs effectively utilize volunteer leadership that may not be available to other educational programs (for example, men with limited Bible knowledge, college students, or retired adults).

Clubs that operate independent of local churches (Young Life or Good News, for instance) may be perceived as competitors by church leaders, though a cooperative relationship can benefit both the congregation and the organization.

Choosing a Program

Three main guidelines help a church choose a Christian club program:

• *Assess the available volunteer base.* A large percentage of Christian clubs flounder, often within two or three years of their beginning, because volunteers are not trained properly and find leadership too demanding. Churches should try to maintain a ratio of one adult leader to no more than eight children. Effective leaders have either been mentored by veterans or formally trained by the club program's professional staff. Club meetings and activities demand that leaders have solid administration skills, a strong commitment to reaching youth for Christ, and the ability to provide group discipline.

• *Count the costs.* Clubs require a financial investment by the church, otherwise all the expenses are borne by the participants. Costs for curriculum materials, awards, uniforms, dues, and craft resources can add up quickly. Most churches attempt to cover leadership expenses and charge club members only for individual costs. A club of 20 to 25 members and several adult volunteers can expect to spend at least $500 annually.

• *Evaluate various club curricula.* Observe how the Bible is used, and don't be misled by the total number of memory verses, a favorite marketing factor. Ask: Are meeting plans outlined for easy use by busy volunteers? Are club activities attractive and meaningful to children? Does the curriculum give adults the opportunity to develop friendships with youth? How complicated is the program for volunteers to operate? How much emphasis is placed on external rewards compared to personal development and relationships?

Selected Christian Clubs

Awana Clubs
  International
1 E. Bode Road
Streamwood, IL 60107

Calvinist Cadet
  Corps/Calvinettes
Box 7259
Grand Rapids, MI 49510

Christian Service Brigade
P.O. Box 150
Wheaton, IL 60189

Girls in Action (SBC)
P.O. Box 830010
Birmingham, AL 35283

Good News Club
Child Evangelism Fellowship
Warrenton, MO 63387

Pioneer Clubs
P.O. Box 788
Wheaton, IL 60189

Royal Ambassadors
1445 Boonville Ave.
Springfield, MO 65802

Word of Life Fellowship
P.O. Box 600
Schroon Lake, NY 12870

Youth for Christ/
  Campus Life
P.O. Box 228822
Denver, CO 80222

Young Life
P.O. Box 520
Colorado Springs, CO 80901
—Paul Heidebrecht

Young-Adult Activities

Young adults are not all alike. In this group, ranging in age from 18 to 28, a church might have college students living on campus or commuting, college-age people working and living at home or away from home, unemployed people anxious to find a job, military personnel, blue-collar workers, executive types, yuppies on the rise, and yuppies on the decline. We might have singles who have never been married and singles who once were, along with young marrieds with children and young marrieds without children, and the unmarried with children. We can have the disabled and those on the comeback trail from drugs, alcohol, illness, or bankruptcy.

Target Your Audience

What we *can't* have very effectively is just one group for everyone of young-adult age! If we are going to minister to young adults, we will need to target our audience by either looking at what kinds of young adults are already in our church or what kinds we'd like to reach. For instance, if a church is near a college campus and has a few students in the congregation, it might want to begin a ministry geared specifically to undergraduate students.

Suppose we survey our commu-

nity and discover that no one is doing anything in the area of divorce recovery (a big young-adult need). We could do more research, gather resources, recruit a leadership team, and begin a six-week course that helps people pick up the pieces after a divorce. As people finish that experience, we might decide to begin a continuing group for them and others in a particular age range. We would now have three separate ministries: a college ministry, a divorce-recovery program, and a group we might call Genesis, for those, say, in their middle to late 20s.

Perhaps a church is near a military base and not near a college. That church could begin a ministry to military folk. At the same time, the church might be near some apartment complexes primarily occupied by young families. If so, it could begin a couples ministry and also set up a support program for young mothers.

One church is near a downtown office park, so instead of doing a college or military ministry, it emphasizes midweek Bible studies and support groups for business people. The point: We can't just throw open the church doors and expect to meet all the needs through one group called Young Adults.

denominations, but that would be inaccurate. In any denomination, some schools are declining while others are growing. Those that continue to grow are serious about their ministry and are giving it their best efforts.

It is important to remember that Sunday school is about teaching people. The administrative structure is important. We need good curriculum materials. And dedicated teachers and workers must be on hand. Working together with the Holy Spirit as the Master Teacher, we can have effective, vibrant Sunday schools today.

—Dennis E. Williams

Resources

Brown, L. 1986. Sunday school standards. Ventura, Cal.: Regal.

Clark, R., L. John, and A. Sloat. 1991. Christian education: Foundations for the future. Chicago: Moody.

Dean, K. 1992. Sunday school handbook. Nashville: Convention Press.

Westing, H. 1980. The super superintendent. Denver: Accent.

Williams, D. 1993. Volunteers for today's church. Grand Rapids: Baker.

Teacher Recruitment

People get excited about ministry; they get scared off by jobs. Here are five recruiting practices that can help potential teachers see teaching as a ministry, while making recruiting itself less of a chore and more of a ministry.

• *Recruit through relationship.* Recruiting basically is matching people with needs. In order to find a good match, however, we need to know the people in the church: what gets them enthused, how they enjoy spending their time, and what their passions and motivations are.

For example, let's say we've noticed a young mother who has been attending church for some time. We may be tempted to ask her to babysit in the nursery. But when we get to know her, we discover she is gifted in relationship skills and has a desire to evangelize. So, instead we might ask her to design a meaningful outreach program for young mothers. We cannot help people find a ministry if we don't know their gifts, abilities, and interests.

• *Tap by team.* A recruiting team represents a variety of interests, backgrounds, gifts, and passions. The best recruiter for a ministry is the person on the team who is closest to that ministry, the person who is the most excited about it. So the person who is enthusiastic about working with second graders is a better recruiter for second-grade teachers than even the pastor. With a team approach, individuals can be delegated to contact prospective teachers for the areas in which they have the most interest.

• *Set the setting.* The recruiting conversation ideally involves sitting down in quiet, comfortable surroundings and sharing the vision, explaining the objectives, spelling out the expectations, and detailing the support we are willing to give. We can ask people what they think they will need to do the job, think through the outline of the course with them, and ask what books, tapes, or other resources would help them prepare for teaching the class.

The recruiting experience should not be a contract negotiation done hurriedly on a Sunday morning, but rather the creation of a partnership between friends, an informal time of thinking and praying together and reaching a decision. We shouldn't say, "Please respond to the terms written on this paper before you leave today." Rather, we want to arrange an informal meeting that conveys "Let's seek the will of God together."

• *Interpret excuses.* Dealing with excuses is one of the most delicate aspects of recruiting. For one thing, "excuses" are sometimes valid reasons. Learning to tell a reason from an excuse is part of the discernment that goes with recruiting.

Confronted with an obvious excuse, we will need to discern whether to take the excuse as a no or change the job description. Sometimes an excuse simply means "I can't make that big of a commitment. If the commitment were smaller, I would consider it." In this case, we may want to break the job into two or three parts, offering the prospective teacher a portion.

No one feels adequate. The apostle Paul didn't feel adequate, Moses didn't feel adequate, and I sure don't feel adequate. But often we can answer an inadequacy excuse by offering the prospective teacher help, training, prayer support, and resources.

• *Delay for discernment.* We should discourage immediate response during the initial conversation. Our job is not to rope people into our program but to help them discern the will of God. We can close with words to the effect, "Let's pray and think about this possibility for the next few days. Then let's get together a week from now and talk again."

—*Roberta Hestenes*

Teacher Training and Support

Virtually all ministers would agree that a key pastoral task is "the equipping of the saints for the work of service" (Eph. 4:12). Since we can't do everything ourselves, we must give significant attention and encouragement to ongoing teacher training. Fortunately, none of us in North America can say we lack training opportunities and ma-

terials. Here are some of the many options available:

• *Curriculum.* If teachers want to improve their skills, the place to start is to study thoroughly the teaching material. A church I know has a particularly good early-childhood department. The coordinator believes it's because the teachers meet together, study the curriculum, and work out ways to apply it to their students.

Most publishing houses employ professional educators who understand learners and design methods to reach them. Volunteer teachers who ignore the curriculum only deprive themselves and their students.

• *Department meetings.* Regular meetings are essential for planning and coordination, but we also can use them to build skills. When workers join together for prayer and program concerns each month, they enhance accountability and encourage fellowship among the team members.

For example, the boys in a church I served wanted a club program, so several men met for training. The club began with much enthusiasm, but after four or five months, something seemed to be missing. As I checked with the program director, I found the men were no longer meeting for training and prayer once the program got going. Each man was simply doing his thing, resulting in a loss of overall direction, teaching skills, and team spirit.

• *Individual training.* In the average college dorm, though some students enjoy studying as a group for exams, others prefer to isolate themselves in the library. In the same way, some teachers benefit greatly from using a correspondence course, a book, or a tape in the privacy of their homes.

Many churches have assembled a library of training books and cassettes for individual use. When teachers are willing to work individually, we can provide the mate-

rials, encourage them, and try to follow up later with "I'm so happy to see you investing personal time in the ministry of teaching."

• *Guest speakers and workshop leaders.* An outside "expert" can inspire and motivate our teachers. By providing opportunities for teachers to hear stimulating educators, we not only give them bits of information to use in their teaching but also renew their enthusiasm for the Lord's work.

We can strengthen an educational program by bringing in a consultant to conduct a Sunday school evaluation, scheduling an evening for teachers to listen to a local expert speak on building self-esteem in children, inviting a Christian education professor from a Bible college to conduct a Saturday morning seminar, scheduling a Walk Through the Bible seminar, or using a publishing-house consultant to help the teachers learn how to use their curriculum.

• *Conventions and seminars.* The cost of outside training opportunities can be significant but is usually well worth it. For instance, when I was a freshman in college, our youth leader took five of us a hundred miles to attend the InterVarsity conference on missions at Urbana. The sessions were meaningful to me, but equally special was the time I spent with my spiritual mentor and the other committed collegians. The same thing can happen with pastors and Sunday school teachers as they drive to weekend seminars with better teaching on their minds.

—*John Cionca*

26

Youth Ministries

T hough the youth group has flourished during the last half of the twentieth century, youth ministry is a rather new phenomenon in the great developments of church history. Christian youth movements were a product of the Industrial Revolution, which took place first in Europe during the late eighteenth century and later in America. The structures of society fundamentally changed when the means of making a living moved from the home to the factory, from the village to the metropolis, from the controls of church and community to the freedom of boarding houses and bars. Parents feared their young people would forget the values of their heritage. Into this spiritual vacuum stepped a variety of youth ministries that attempted to pass Christian convictions from one generation to the next.

Many strategies were formulated at the grassroots level for the purpose of nurturing the children of the church and evangelizing children from lower socioeconomic levels of the community. Friendly societies, mutual-improvement societies, Sunday school teachers' meetings, singing schools (the forerunners of today's church choirs), temperance and missionary societies, literary and devotional societies—all provided safe places where boys and girls could meet Christian peers.

The birth of the Society for Christian Endeavor in 1881 was the genesis of the modern youth group. Its structure still provides the skeleton upon which the meat and muscle of modern young people's fellowships are supported today.

The denominational youth organizations, which emerged during the last two decades of the nineteenth century, and the parachurch youth ministries, which reached young people for Christ a half century later, flourished and then settled into comfortable patterns of ministry.

Yet one question needs to be asked: Has there been any continuity in youth ministry since its beginnings? In other words, is there anything in youth ministry over the past two centuries that appears to contribute consistently to success? The answer is a resounding Yes! Here are a few basic principles that have insured effective youth ministry across generational, socioeconomic, and cultural barriers.

Enter the Student's World

The most basic principle of youth work—making contact—has been described in many ways. "Contact work," "earning the right to be heard," "building relationships," and "incarnation ministry" are some of the most common descriptions. The cornerstone principle is that youth ministry begins when a spiritually mature adult finds a comfortable way to enter a student's world. Francis Clark made contact with young people through the structured meetings of Christian Endeavor. Jim Rayburn showed up at athletic events, talked with young athletes on their own turf, won their confidence, and eventually invited them to Young Life clubs. David Wilkerson showed up at a police station in the Bronx on behalf of members of a street gang, and from this contact was born Teen Challenge.

Consider these four distinctives of the contact principle:

• *An emphasis on Christian ministry.* Many worthwhile activities benefit young people, and many sponsoring organizations share a Judeo-Christian value system. The goal of Christian youth ministry, however, is fulfilling the Great Commission, which includes both evangelizing and discipling. Without this dual emphasis, youth ministry degenerates into mere youth work.

• *Leadership by spiritually mature adults.* Though some youth movements have been student led initially (for example, the Student Volunteer Movement and the Student Foreign Missions Fellowship), the continuity of vision and leadership over the long haul has always been in the hands of people older than the young people the movements have served. Where youth ministry has been effective, it has had adult leaders who were secure in their relationship with God and with other people. For such people, youth ministry is not a method of prolonging one's adolescence but a mission of helping youth in their spiritual journeys.

To provide this type of attention to the discipleship process, the ratio between leaders and students needs to be at least one adult for every ten young people. Student leadership is not negated by the adults who are involved in youth ministry; it is enhanced. The adult serves as a coach, while the young person calls the signals and leads the team on the field of play.

• *Activities that are mutually comfortable to student and adult.* Mutual interests most frequently provide a point of contact between students and adults. Music, drama, sports, service activities, camping opportunities, Bible quiz teams, ski trips, and weekly youth group meetings all provide environments in which youth and adults can get acquainted and grow to like each other. Only after the comfort level has been established can evangelism or discipleship take place.

• *Ministry that takes place in the student's world.* Just as the Son of God left the splendor of eternity to become incarnate in the hostile world of fallen humanity, so Christian adults must be willing to take the risk of leaving their comfort zones to become pilgrims in a new world. The people in this world are usually more familiar with current musical groups, professional athletes, and TV celebrities than they are with Moses, David, or the apostle Paul. For many adults this initial plunge into the land of youth is akin to a jarring cross-cultural experience.

Lovingly Confront with the Gospel

To enter a student's world, as difficult as it is for many adults, is only the beginning of youth ministry. The most significant part of the ministry equation emerges when young people are lovingly confronted with biblical truth and its implications in their lives. Adolescents are attempting to become their own people. They are sorting out what convictions they hold and what standards they reject. To become mature, youth will take frequent opportunities to reject the convictions of the adults who surround them—parents, teachers, pastors, doctors, and even police.

Youth-ministry people stand between the generations, imploring the old to understand the young and the young to appreciate their elders. Such ministers stand in the gap, holding out the Word of Life. To enter a student's world without teaching him or her to view the world through the lens of Christian conviction hints at personal or spiritual immaturity on the part of the adult leader. It takes skill and conviction to induce students to confront themselves in the light of biblical truth.

Confrontation in youth ministry seldom means preaching at passive learners. Though preaching is appropriate in many settings, most of the time students need to discover biblical values through both a social and biblical process of induction. They need to discover, experiment with, and eventually internalize biblical truth. Youth groups, from their beginning, have been places where students could come to grips with the Christian values of their parents' generation.

With what should the young person be confronted? The Christian gospel is the core message, with all of its implications for salvation, personal lifestyle, interpersonal relationships, and stewardship of God's creation.

There is a danger, however, for youth ministers as they confront students with the gospel. Some expect youth to respond as adults might respond, failing to account for the maturing process that has happened in their own lives during the ensuing years since adolescence. In frustration at the lack of adequate response, Christian youth leaders may resort to manipulative tactics to produce "results." Seldom are these strategies effective in bringing the freedom of the gospel to young people.

Junior High Ministries

Junior high kids are special. Caught in a whirlpool of change, they are growing and developing in every area of life as they transform from children into young adults. *Physically*, limbs and bodies seem to gain inches and pounds overnight, and adult hormones kick in, bringing new sexual awareness. *Socially*, junior highers aggressively seek out friendships, with the phone becoming a social ally and a constant companion.

Mentally, early adolescents navigate the uneasy path from the concrete to the conceptual, viewing life mostly in black-and-white tones; things are "excellent" or "stupid." *Emotionally*, junior highers experience great highs, followed by rapid descent into deep lows. Their psycho-emotional focus is on competence—learning new skills in order to answer the questions "What can I do?" and "What am I good at?"

Spiritually, these kids begin to question what they've been taught in Sunday school. Church isn't considered "cool" in junior high, and many young teens stop attending church as soon as they can manage it with their parents.

Reaching Junior Highers

Unfortunately, during these difficult years, just when they most need mature guidance, faithful relationships, and overt expressions of love, junior highers are sometimes deserted or ignored. They tend to fall into a ministry gap—stuck between the children (with their colorful and creative programs and Christmas pageants) and the senior highers (with their full-time, professional youth worker).

Junior highers do need lots of love and attention. Here's how to reach and help them.

● *Provide positive adult role models.* Junior high students still look up to adults. They will respect those who respect them and follow those

Develop a Delivery System

Youth for Christ rallies and, later, Campus Life clubs, Fellowship of Christian Athletes' huddle groups and conferences, Young Life clubs and camps, denominational youth programs (such as Free Church Youth Fellowship, Lutheran Youth fellowship, Royal Ambassadors, and Young Calvinist Federation) are examples of youth ministry delivery systems. A delivery system is an organized means of getting students from the point of contact to the moments of confrontation with the Christian gospel.

Competition, humor, skits, testimonies of Christian personalities, discussions, concerts, and a host of other program elements can move students from a casual commitment to an adult or peers to a serious consideration of the gospel message. While dozens of models of youth

who spend time with them. Parents can make excellent volunteers, because most junior highers still enjoy having Mom and Dad around.

• *Give them a safe place.* Every event and program should provide a safe haven where kids feel affirmed, where they can experience success instead of failure. Leaders should allow no name calling or belittling, and games should give everyone an equal chance to win.

• *Relate the Bible to life.* Kids reared in church know the Bible stories; now they need to sense the Bible's relevance to life, *real* life. Otherwise they will discard the faith with their childhood toys. Teach junior highers how to read, understand, and apply the Bible. Make Christianity practical to their growing and changing world.

• *Exercise discipline.* Early adolescents seem squirrelly and out of control—because they usually are! Often when they act up, they can hardly help it. They need well-defined rules and limits administered by adults who will firmly and kindly enforce those rules. A stern look,

a hand on the shoulder, or a quiet but direct "That is not acceptable" communicates concern for the individual as well as the group.

• *Teach life skills.* Because junior highers want and need to learn "how to," this is the ideal time to teach them how to succeed in life. Design or find lessons that teach "How to Make Friends," "How to Get Along with the Opposite Sex," "How to Get What You Need," "How to Resolve Conflicts," and other clearly relevant topics. Also include spiritual-life skills such as "How to Pray," "How to Worship," and "How to Explain What You Believe." Teach these skills by following three simple steps: explanation, demonstration, and supervision (active practicing).

• *Have fun.* Filled with boundless energy, junior highers are fun, and they like to have fun. In fact, two sixth-grade boys can spend hours chasing each other around the yard or family room. Laugh with them, play with them, and enjoy life with them.

—Dave Veerman

God. There is no truth apart from the person or actions of God. All truth is God's truth, without division into so-called "sacred truth" and "secular truth." Such a division indicates faulty thinking about the nature of God as Creator of all that exists, including history and mathematics, science and language, music and the arts. Jesus Christ is to be the center of all learning and living, because in him "are hidden all the treasures of wisdom and knowledge" (Col. 2:3).

Yet there is a basic, critical difference between the Christian and the secular *approaches* to education. The facts of knowledge are identical for both to explore. The difference is in the interpretation of those facts. The Christian school purposes to integrate facts with the Word of God, believing that no subject can be understood in totality when the Creator-Savior is ignored or denied. The secular approach to education teaches facts but omits God. The integration of a God-centered world-view with a sound academic curriculum need not be strained or forced in the Christian school but can be natural, "for in him we live and move and have our being" (Acts 17:28).

● *Life has a divine purpose and a moral design.* Everyone involved in launching a Christian school must be convinced that human beings are to live their lives as a response to their Creator-Savior, enjoying him and endeavoring to please him through doing justly, loving mercy, and walking humbly with him. The eternal state of each human being is determined by that person's response to the call of God in Christ Jesus.

It follows that the absolute determination of what is morally right or wrong is the prerogative of God alone, revealed to us in his Word, both written (the Bible) and living (Jesus). Since the Holy Spirit indwells every Christian and he convicts us of sin, guides us into all truth, and magnifies Christ, we can agree to accept the values for life that are derived from the Word of God.

Setting the Student Objectives

The goals of Christian school education rest on the philosophical underpinnings stated above. Building on these broad statements, school planners can begin working on specific teaching and learning objectives for the students. These will no doubt include, at the least, foundational statements such as these:

● *The Bible will be presented as the basis for the most fulfilling life.* Students not only should be taught what the Bible says but should learn how to study it for themselves. Bible content is best taught in a devotional manner, so students learn to be open-hearted and affected by the revelation of God's will for their daily lives. This approach fosters the best kind of character development, in which students are growing into the likeness of Christ.

With the Bible as the foundation, the teaching of related truths naturally follows. Students are encouraged to receive Jesus Christ as Savior and Lord, the master of their lives. Through an ever-deepening commitment, they are encouraged to become disciples who submit themselves to his direction throughout their lives. In addition, biblical standards of morality and ethics are set forth as absolute truth, not relative. They are presented as God's standards for our good in this life. The lifelong objectives of doing justly, loving mercy, and walking humbly with God are presented as reachable goals, not as mere idealistic visions.

• *Care for the human welfare of others will be cultivated.* Students are shown how to relate to non-Christians and to Christians who hold differing points of views. Involvement in practical ways with world missions—and with local missions projects for the hungry and homeless—is set forth as urgent. Students are taught to pray for their neighbors and their world, seeking practical ways to get involved with the needs of those around them.

The Pastor-Administrator Relationship

A church school is best administered when the personal relationship between pastor and administrator is strong and amicable. The pastor should be confident that the administrator is well-qualified for the job and is to give the administrator the freedom to do it.

Keeping Strong Relationships

Unless the administrator can independently lead the school in a way that reflects the church's beliefs and complements its ministry, both institutions will suffer. Here are some essential requirements for an effective pastor-administrator relationship. They'll need:

• *Theological compatibility.* Compatibility on theological beliefs and on the principles of daily living is essential, since both the administrator and pastor offer spiritual leadership. Since the pastor is the administrator's pastor, however, the administrator should experience him or her as understanding and open to different points of view.

• *A respect for separate ministries.* The pastor needs a strong, genuine commitment to the ministry of the school, seeing that the school gets proper visibility in the church and that the administrator is recognized for leadership. At the same time, the administrator is responsible to provide adequate data, so the pastor can feel comfortable discussing the school with any audience.

• *Public solidarity.* It's best for the administrator to have a specific, visible ministry in church on Sundays. The pastor should speak in chapel periodically and to the

● *The knowledge and skills required for higher education, occupational competence, and lifelong learning will be taught.* The school should work at developing young minds that can be discriminating and wise throughout the whole of life. Students are encouraged to perform to the limits of individual ability in ways that test and push back personal intellectual boundaries. In other words, students would be encouraged to stretch their minds to full capacity from early childhood through adulthood, becoming lifelong learners who continue learning as the world itself changes.

Students are taught to think courageously and to stand up for their spiritual beliefs under pressure, as they learn to study and to work independently and cooperatively. Communication skills, creative skills, and proficiency in music, art, and drama would be developed, along with physical education that stresses wholesome, lifelong recreational participation.

● *The importance of personal, civic responsibility will be enhanced by the school's activities.* Christian schools should be in the business of

---

faculty as well, while the administrator should participate in the meetings of the church staff.

Both need to build up the other in public contacts. They should be open with each other and friendly, scheduling time to pray and talk together at least once a week. Problems arising between them need to be resolved directly and immediately, without defensiveness, because each desires the Lord's will.

● *A commitment to loyalty.* When approached about a problem concerning the other person or that person's domain of responsibility, they should support and defend the other's integrity by getting the reporting party to go directly to their colleague to solve the matter.

If the pastor is also a parent in the school, he or she must never pull rank on behalf of the children. Pastors need to observe the same rules and work through the same channels as any other parent.

● *A plan for decision making.* The administrator should be allowed to make independent decisions, keeping the pastor informed and asking for counsel so that such decisions will not be contrary to the overall ministry goals. However, the pastor dare not become overinvolved with the school to the detriment of pastoral work or the work of the administrator. There should be a balance, a symmetry. This requires a deepening of the relationship, so the trust level remains high.

There is wisdom in having the church board supervise the administrator, yet the pastor must have direct access to the administrator without going through the board. This would be pastoral access rather than administrative, however. The pastor is not to go above the board or around it for administrative purposes.

—*Roy W. Lowrie, Jr.*

developing good citizens, in light of the apostle Paul's teachings in Romans 13. Civic participation should be taught, encouraged, and modeled by the school staff, who demonstrate how Christians can live faithfully in their culture, being in the world but not of the world.

Teachers would emphasize cultural heritage and the need to find solutions to the serious issues facing the country and the world. This is done in light of the centrality of the healthy family as established by God. Biblical precepts would be conveyed for the present and for the future when students marry and establish their own homes, all based on the biblical call to view life as sacred.

Financial Support for Christian Schools

It is better to build children than to repair adults. Perhaps that is why private Christian schools are springing up all across America. How to fund these schools, though, is the big question school founders and administrators are continually asking.

Spiritual Foundations

Building on a firm spiritual foundation is crucial, because it takes a miracle in our present economy to find sufficient money to pay for private education! Only God can perform miracles, but we human beings can participate in those miracles. The key is to find out what God is doing, translate God's will into a clear vision we can interpret to others, and then identify with God in the work he is doing. We can then expect the winds of heaven to drive us on to success.

Naturally, along with a spiritual foundation of prayer and seeking God's will for funding our schools, we must offer a product that parents desire for their children. They invariably want a wholesome Christian environment and quality education with high academic standards. So the curriculum itself must have a spiritual foundation. It is important to teach basic Christian truths and ethics along with all the cultural subjects that will enhance the capacity of children to enjoy full lives. Regular chapels also build a worshiping community.

Sources of Funding

Once we have laid the spiritual foundations and made plans to offer a well-rounded, quality education, we must gain the enrollment numbers to fund the program through tuitions.

In the early 1990s, the average tuition for independent Christian schools was $3–4,000 a year. Tuitions for independent schools are usually higher than those for church-sponsored schools because the independents must buy land and build buildings. Church-related schools using facilities provided by the church can often reduce fees

Defining the School-Church Relationship

Schools that are thoroughly integrated into the ministry of the church have the fewest problems. But problems that can occur without a close, highly communicative relationship might include tension between Christian-school students and secular-school students together in Sunday school and the youth group, an elder board that is not unified in its endorsement and support of the school, and public-school teachers in the congregation who may begin to feel the Christian-school supporters are subtly indicting their work. In addition, a

---

by approximately one-third, making the tuition about $2,000 per year on the average.

A rule of thumb in budgeting is a third of income for salaries, a third for operational costs, and a third for land and buildings. Adequate enrollment numbers are necessary to provide sufficient funding. I have found good results in designing facilities for 900 students.

Approximately 80 percent of the funds to run a private school will come from tuitions and fees. The remaining 20 percent can come from various sources. Here are some revenue sources to tap:

- *Matching funds.* Hundreds of corporations are willing to give matching funds through their employees (the parents of the students). These companies typically promise to give—dollar for dollar—the same amount an employee gives to the school. Matching funds can speed classroom construction and equipment purchases during the beginning of a new school.

- *Grandparents.* Consider holding a Grandparents' Day, inviting these folks to the school to visit their grandchildren's classrooms. Discuss the program and needs of the school in a large-group meeting and appeal for grandparents' financial support.

- *Capital drives.* Make a practice of running a capital-fund drive once every two years. Call upon donation-capable parents to help meet the capital needs of the school.

- *Foundations.* In California alone, there are about forty foundations that might be interested in supporting special programs, such as building a computer lab or a vocational workshop. We simply need to find out how to apply for funds— and then ask.

- *Memorials.* Make a list of needs, such as classroom furnishings, science and computer equipment, and playground structures. Certain parents will appreciate the opportunity to give a memorial in the name of a deceased loved one. Attach tastefully designed nameplates to the equipment.

- *Philanthropic gifts.* Invite qualified people who are capable of giving large gifts to become members of your school board. Acquaint them with the benefits of private Christian education and with the larger capital needs of the school. Many will be happy to offer their financial support.

—Ernest D. Sillers

significant problem can arise if people begin to believe Christian-
school education is the primary church priority or that it is the only
way for children to grow in Christ and develop spiritually. Then the
broad ministry of the body of Christ for mutual edification is down-
graded.

To avoid dissension in the church, the pastor has to deal continu-
ously with the ebb and flow of church members' attitudes toward the
school. Some will always strongly oppose it, and others will always
faithfully support it.

The following insights regarding issues in the school-church relationship were contributed by pastors who are strong proponents of
the Christian school and have a demonstrated commitment to its welfare. But each also acknowledges that there have been problems for
his ministry caused by the school. Understanding and wisdom permeate their observations.

• *The school and pastoral involvement.* Without good, open communication between members of the church and school staffs, problems
will arise for the pastor. There also will be a significant problem if the
school begins taking the minister's time and energy away from pastoral tasks and priorities. Unfortunately, the pastor may have chosen—
to the detriment of the church—to be more involved in the school
administration than is prudent, thereby neglecting the church. It's no
secret that the school can be demanding; the pastor, however, must
have the utmost confidence in the school administrator and govern-
ing board.

Pastors must be on guard about subtle dangers to their church ministry: The school can drain leadership away from the church, especially if the church is small; the school increases the pastor's
counseling load because school parents who go to other churches
come to the school pastor for counseling; and interpersonal problems
between parents, teachers, and administrators can quickly sap the
pastor's emotional energy.

• *Enrollment from church members.* Here's a grievous problem for
the church leadership: Encouraging high numbers of students from
the church to enroll in the Christian school can actually keep families
whose children attend other schools from coming to the church! This
fact makes necessary a different kind of program for youth—all the
youth in the community, whether they are involved with the Christian school or not.

Another problem in this area relates to who is qualified for school
leadership. One rule of thumb is that church members not enrolling
their children in the school should not be given positions of authority
in the school. This is similar to rules requiring an elder or deacon to
be a church member.

• *Financial responsibility and accountability.* Developing financial stability for the school is critical and requires great care. The handling of money is a spiritual matter, demanding that salaries, fringe benefits, raises, and vacation time be made equitable among the school and church staff. Yet, the most potentially divisive question will be: How large should the school become in terms of constructing new buildings and investing additional church monies?

The student-teacher ratio is the biggest single factor in financing the school. The cost of tuition needs balance, so that it is not so low that the church acquires a monumental bailout burden each year and not so high that all but the financially elite are priced out of the market. Tuition should cover faculty and staff salaries and fringe benefits, usually about 80 percent of the budget.

Preparing for the Future

As we approach the new century, more students are enrolled in Christian schools than at any time in the nation's history. As the secularization of public schools continues, Christian schools based upon the Bible are increasing in number and in size. This relationship is a striking phenomenon: Cultural decadence appears to stimulate Christian growth! At the same time, there is an ebb and flow of enrollment in individual Christian schools, depending on local and national issues. Also, the regions of the country vary in their rate of growth.

As we look to the future, we see that the Christian-school movement confronts challenges similar to those of churches, mission boards, and other Christian endeavors, such as: (1) keeping the vision bright, (2) finding good leadership, (3) obtaining adequate financing, (4) maintaining quality facilities, and (5) creating effective internal and external public relations.

Christian schools will continue to have problems, as will churches. Small Christian secondary schools experience the most difficult challenges of all, often making their very survival problematic. Yet the results of this educational ministry in the lives of students and families are worth the sacrifices involved in resolving the problems. A typical testimony written by a parent said, "The school strengthens the Christian foundation of our home. Our entire family has grown and matured from this experience."

Churches interested in starting a Christian school need to consider these brief but basic guidelines:

• *Seek legal counsel.* Do this right at the outset of the planning process. Get ongoing advice from an educational lawyer whose work has been with Christian schools.

• *Take the time to hire the right staff.* It's crucial, for example, to hire a proficient administrator, since the head of the school is the linchpin of the entire enterprise. The school exists for the students, and they deserve qualified teachers who are assigned to their major fields of study.

• *Seek staff input on construction plans.* Have the administrator and teachers work with a school architect in designing or adapting facilities. Work to design church educational facilities to *school* specifications. A congregation never knows when it might need to use supposedly church-only spaces for dayschool purposes.

• *Start a school only if you believe in it with all your heart.* And, incidentally, a pastor's level of commitment to the school will no doubt be judged by whether or not his or her children are enrolled.

—*Roy W. Lowrie, Jr.*

Resources

Enderlin, A., and R. White, eds. 1986. The manual of administration for new and young Christian schools. Whittier, Cal.: Association of Christian Schools International.

Gaebelein, F. 1985. The pattern of God's truth. Winona Lake, Ind.: BMH Books.

Kienel, P., ed. 1978. Philosophy of Christian school education. Whittier, Cal.: Association of Christian Schools International.

Knight, G. 1989. Issues and alternatives in educational philosophies, 2d ed. Berrien Springs, Mich.: Andrews University Press.

Teachers and Staff

The effectiveness of any Christian school rises and falls with two vital factors: philosophy and staff. The school that is founded on strong biblical principles and hires the right people to carry out that biblical philosophy will certainly be the dynamic school God desires.

Any school striving for spiritual academic excellence must set high standards when seeking school employees. If a school board becomes nervous and quickly hires someone to fill a position for fear they may not find another candidate, they often will regret such haste later. On the other hand, the school that is willing to be patient in searching for the best candidate will usually be blessed with God's choice.

Staffing Guidelines

Here are specific suggestions to keep in mind when seeking to hire and retain the right teachers and staff:

• *Bathe hiring decisions in prayer.* Luke 6:12 gives us an excellent personnel principle. Here Jesus spends the entire night in prayer, and the next day, from among all his disciples, he chooses twelve to be his close apostles. We must exercise great caution against hiring in a hurry, especially if chance circumstances happen to bring potential employees to the school.

• *Interview thoroughly.* During the interview all major concerns should be covered, namely: philosophy of the school, standards and expectations for students and staff, and evaluation procedures for workers. Salary and related fringe benefits should naturally be covered in proper detail.

Employers make a major mistake by presenting only the most positive image and skipping sensitive or negative issues. It is best to present a perfectly honest, clear picture of the job situation.

• *Streamline the hiring process.* Once candidates are located, implement a simple procedure from interview to hiring. All of the regular hiring steps, such as the detailed interview, careful assessment of past performance, and proper reference checks must be followed for each candidate. We must realize, however, that often good people are lost because the process is too long and cumbersome. For example, if a strong prospect is asked to change an interview date several times because the committee can't get together, this person easily could change her mind about accepting the position.

• *Don't overlook the most obvious sources of candidates.* Sources for staff prospects may be right next door. We should include in our search the church body where the school is housed, local churches that are in harmony doctrinally, and colleges and seminaries that may be located nearby.

• *Don't dictate exactly how the job is to be done.* A common error is to carefully and prayerfully hire the right person and then turn around and handcuff that person, almost making it appear as if the new employee is under suspicion. This type of job environment causes the new person to be tentative, lacking creativity.

There is nothing wrong with providing training sessions for new workers. Many assignments, however, can stand some new approaches, and employees should be encouraged to find them.

• *Don't neglect regular reviews.* A mutually developed evaluation system is one of the best motivators. When workers feel they are appreciated by their supervisors, they will be happy. Therefore, we need to offer evaluation conferences once or twice a year. (In the difficult times when a staff member may have to be dismissed, these conferences also can be a source of documentation of the problem.)

In harmony with the Bible's sowing and reaping principle, if a school treats each employee fairly and kindly, regardless of position, God in turn usually blesses that ministry with good workers.

—*Art Nazigian*

School Facilities

One of the most deeply challenging ministries a church can undertake is starting a Christian school. The need for Christian schools grows by the day with humanism increasing around us. As a church earnestly prays and seeks God's will about starting a school, it must, at the same time, assess its facilities to see if they are adequate.

Questions Needing Answers

What does a church need to know before determining what facilities to provide? Or how will it assess whether present facilities can adequately house the Monday school? Answers to the following questions should have a major impact on faculty decisions.

● *What grade levels will the school provide?* Most churches that have or are starting a Christian school begin with the first three or four grades. They add one or two grades each year thereafter until the grade that completes the school is reached. It is not difficult to launch a school that will eventually cover grades K–8. The greatest amount of effort is involved when the church wants to have a quality high school.

The cost of a high school program is about three times greater than that of an elementary program. Having 20 to 24 students in a class will cover the expenses of an elementary classroom, including the teacher's salary. In high school, however, the classes are much smaller, and there are many more classes to choose from, thus driving per-pupil costs much higher.

● *What will be the class size limits?* Ideally, for elementary school (grades K–6), classrooms that provide for 30 square feet per child are standard. This space allows for the basic educational needs, such as areas for doing small-committee work, a reading corner, a science center, a closet, and storage areas. For example, a class of 20 students should have a classroom at least 20 feet by 30 feet in size.

The floor space needed for junior and senior high is only 20 square feet per student, since less physical activity will take place in the room. Churches that may not have this recommended floor space can still meet minimal requirements, provided classrooms are well lighted and ventilated, with at least ten square feet per student.

● *What is the political climate for permits?* Securing a permit or approval to operate a Christian school in a church is generally not difficult, since, presumably, the church already is conducting a safe and proper Sunday school. However, it is always wise to check with the proper officials to be sure you aren't overlooking any major building codes or other requirements for running a weekly school program.

● *Will we have a library?* The "facility heart" of the school is its library. One of the largest, most attractive, centrally located rooms should serve as the library and the multimedia center. All films, audio and video cassettes, computers, and other like equipment can also be housed in this room.

● *Will we offer special courses?* Does the school plan to provide art, music, or physical education classes? For high school programs, science and computer centers are essential, and churches will need to single out the larger rooms to accommodate these two subject areas. The type and quantity of science equipment and materials will determine the size of the room needed. Students and teachers must take extreme safety precautions when doing chemical experiments, so running water, excellent ventilation, and easy-access fire exits are absolute necessities when setting up the science room.

—Art Nazigian

Preschools

Naturally, the first step in organizing a preschool is to canvass the church, neighborhood, and community to assess the need for such a program. This assessment will also provide information about the specific type of child the school might serve, particularly whether the program will be limited to church children or include other children in the community. A congregation also begins to see potential students' needs through this assessment activity.

Six Steps to a School

If the assessment effort shows the need for a preschool program, at least six subsequent steps are in order:

• *Hire a professional consultant.* It's wise to engage the services of a competent preschool consultant, at least during the initial creation and organization of the school. Each state has strict regulations, and the consultant will contact the proper state and local departments to learn those regulations and see that they are implemented. A consultant will also evaluate the potential facilities to determine whether they comply with government regulations and support school goals. The consultant can also lead the church through each of the subsequent steps, saving valuable time and expenses.

• *Set up a board.* The school board will provide essential support for the director and staff. Describe, in minute detail, the roles and responsibilities of the school

board members. The board could be composed of parents, members of the church, people elected by the church membership, or people appointed by a church board. They must be individuals of high moral standing in the community and thoroughly dedicated to childhood education. They need not be professional educators but must be open to learning everything they can about the schooling task.

• *State your educational philosophy.* This philosophical statement will determine the school's overall mission. Include descriptive statements about the nature of the preschool child, the reason for learning at this age level, and the course of the maturation process. Identify the mission, goals, and specific objectives of the school. Define the roles of both the learner and the teacher. Address the relevant biblical issues related to spiritual growth as well as academic learning. A statement of philosophy provides the rationale upon which all future decisions will be made.

• *Develop the budget.* This initial financial statement should include startup expenditures, employee costs, rent, health insurance, taxes, scholarships, the cost of equipment and instructional materials, and other items peculiar to the specific school. Identify income sources with the estimated amounts to be received. Possible sources of income include tuition, grants, fundraising projects, gifts, and church subsidies. Obviously, there should be adequate income to meet projected expenses.

• *Design the curriculum.* The educational objectives and curriculum design flow from the philosophical statement. Educational objectives should speak to the three basic areas of learning: cognitive, affective, and psychomotor. The curriculum should also consider the social and personal needs of the child. The 3- or 4-year-old child learns primarily through doing, and all learning activities should be based on this fact.

Preschool leaders can contact established Christian school organizations to obtain information about instructional materials that integrate faith and learning. Two national associations are Christian Schools International (Grand Rapids, Michigan) and the Association of Christian Schools International (Whittier, California).

• *Staff the program.* Identify the staff to fill, such as director, head teacher, teachers, cook, nurse, janitor, and bus driver. For each position, determine the credentials needed and write a detailed job description before interviewing and hiring the candidates who best fit the school's needs and philosophy.

—*John A. Burgess*

Part VII:

Chaplaincies

I t's tough to be a pastor on someone else's turf. But every day, thousands of clergy provide pastoral care in decidedly unchurchly situations—dusty military compounds, frantic hospital emergency rooms, down-and-dirty cell blocks, and speeding patrol cars. Some pastors live out their faith and their calling in the oddest of places—much like the kinds of places in which Jesus placed himself during his earthly ministry.

While the functions of ministry remain similar in these places, the rules are often different. There are questions of command and authority. Role conflicts arise more easily. Church-state policies thrust themselves to the fore. Loneliness and professional isolation eat at chaplains. People don't know what category to place them in, and so they're the oddity, the unusual agents in most situations.

But amid such struggles, ministry continues. The Word gets preached on the poop deck, in pediatrics, and at the police officer's funeral. Counsel is given on death row, at a crime scene, and in the ICU. Teaching is communicated under a camouflage canopy, in a hospital conference room, and at a work-farm Bible study. Captive audiences and begrudging respect are part of the mix for chaplains.

To keep chaplains from being the Lone Rangers on the frontiers of Christian ministry, congregations have a supportive role to play. And parish pastors can stand beside chaplains of all kinds, even serving as volunteer chaplains in many situations. The main idea is that all people need ministry, even those in unusual circumstances. For their benefit, the following advice is offered.

29

Military Chaplains

The military chaplaincy predates both the U.S. Constitution and the Declaration of Independence. The origin of the U.S. military chaplaincy is generally traced to an action by the Continental Congress on July 29, 1775, which authorized a pay scale for army chaplains. While chaplains had served in British units and on board ship, this congressional action was the earliest official legislative recognition of chaplains as a part of the U.S. military establishment. Appointments of chaplains to the Continental Navy soon followed, and by 1777 chaplains were serving in large numbers in both services.

Interestingly, many chaplains who served in the Revolutionary War were also active combatants. Some even led troops into battle. Not until later in military history were chaplains considered noncombatants. In the early days, few chaplains saw any conflict between the roles of clergyperson and combat soldier. Over the years chaplains came to enjoy a reputation in the services as courageous guardians of moral, ethical, and spiritual truth.

The Nature of the Chaplaincy

The unique status of the military chaplain as a staff officer serving on the personal staff of the commander presents both a challenge and an opportunity. According to Army regulations, chaplains are "expected to speak with a prophetic voice" and to "confront the command when the religious rights of soldiers are affected." It is this

445

requirement to be an integral part of the command that sets chaplains apart from other clergy or lay persons that carry on ministry with the military community. Access is the key. Being a part of the unit, living with and working with service members, the chaplain has the opportunity to be salt and light to an entire community.

• *Becoming a chaplain.* The educational and physical requirements for appointment as a military chaplain have changed little during the past 40 years. Since chaplains are commissioned as officers in the armed services, they must be physically and morally fit. They must meet the educational standards for other officers (a bachelor's degree) and must also have completed three years of resident theological education at an approved seminary. A Master of Divinity degree or equivalent is required prior to appointment.

Furthermore, chaplains must be endorsed by their respective denominations and then serve at the pleasure of their denominational bodies. Should a chaplain be at odds with his or her church body or unresponsive to its discipline, that church body may withdraw its endorsement and recall the chaplain to civilian life. When this occurs, the service terminates the chaplain's commission, and he or she is released from military service.

The services do not evaluate chaplains on theological or ecclesiological grounds, nor do they train them in those areas. Chaplains are brought into the services based on formulas designed to ensure an equitable distribution by denominational affiliation. While the services do not use a quota system, they do try to maintain a "faith balance" within each service. Once chaplains enter the armed services, they are treated as other officers in terms of promotions and assignments, except that they are separately managed by the respective Chiefs of Chaplains.

• *Serving as a chaplain.* The rank structure of the three service chaplaincies parallels that of the regular armed services. Chaplains begin their ministries as First Lieutenants (Army and Air Force) or Lieutenants, Junior Grade (Navy) but are usually promoted in a year or less to Captain (Army and Air Force) or Lieutenant (Navy). After three years of service, they are selected for continuation for an initial indefinite term.

At about the six-year mark, they are eligible for selection to the next higher grade. If promoted to Major (Army and Air Force) or Lieutenant Commander (Navy), they are then integrated into the regular force and, barring a disciplinary or behavioral problem, can continue to serve for at least 20 years. If promoted to Lieutenant Colonel (Army and Air Force) or Commander (Navy), they can serve for 28 years. If selected for Colonel (Army and Air Force) or Captain (Navy), they can serve a full 30 years or longer. Two senior chaplain officers are selected from each service for promotion to the rank of Brigadier and Major

General (Army and Air Force) or Rear Admiral (Navy) to serve as Chiefs and Deputy Chiefs of Chaplains in their respective services.

Service as a chaplain requires keeping two seemingly conflicting responsibilities in healthy tension. On the one hand, chaplains are public servants, paid by the government to minister to all personnel. On the other hand, as ordained clergy they must remain true to their ordination vows and particular theological distinctives. Fortunately, the services make allowances for this, and chaplains are not required to participate in activities or perform duties contrary to the tenets of their faith traditions. This important understanding is essential to the chaplain's performance in the military environment. The key words are "cooperation without compromise."

• *Maintaining professional status.* As commissioned officers, chaplains are expected to meet and maintain the standards of a highly trained, elite group. At the same time they must be able to relate to the most junior and sometimes immature service members. However, in so doing, they cannot compromise their professional status. Commanders at all levels expect their chaplains not only to set a high moral, ethical, and spiritual tone, but also to exhibit competence and professionalism in their work. Often, chaplains are judged not by how well they do as pastors but by how well they perform as professional staff officers.

Although wearing two hats (or serving two masters) presents a challenge to the chaplain, the professional status conferred upon him or her can also be of great value when it comes to communicating the gospel and penetrating the military system. The chaplain speaks with the authority of both church and state as an insider. If the chaplain has cultivated and maintains good relations with the command leadership, he or she can exert a profound influence for good. On the other hand, some chaplains are co-opted by the system and end up muting their message and compromising their values in order to get ahead.

Duties and Responsibilities

Chaplains have a unique opportunity to exercise influence not only through their ministry to individuals but also as they speak to the institution. As staff officers, chaplains often participate in the decision-making process, bringing a moral-ethical-spiritual perspective to the internal debate on strategy, tactics, or operations. Thus, chaplains serve as prophetic voices, bringing a "word from the Lord" to the most secular of discussions. In this sense, when obedient to their calling, they are indeed salt and light.

• *Religious duties.* While military chaplains are essentially pastors, priests, or rabbis carrying on religious ministry, the diversity and extent of their religious duties set them apart from civilian clergy. First, they are required by law to conduct public worship services and burial services for members of the command to which they are assigned. While they may normally conduct denominationally distinctive worship services, when ministering to the community at large, chaplains must provide opportunity for all service members to worship. They need not *conduct* services inconsistent with the tenets of their faith, but they must *provide* such services for their people.

Further, chaplains are expected to administer sacraments, ordinances, and ministrations upon request. They are expected to participate in military and patriotic ceremonies, provide pastoral care (including visitation and in-depth counseling), and supervise or conduct religious education for service members and their families.

While there are areas of specialization within the overall chaplaincy

---

Authority and Conscience

The year was 1967. The place was Vietnam. Members of a Special Forces unit were on a search-and-destroy mission deep in Vietcong-controlled jungle territory. Continually harassed by sniper fire from an elusive enemy, these soldiers were on edge, their nerves raw. The commander's jeep driver, a young soldier of good reputation, well liked by both his compatriots and his commander, had gone down to the nearby stream to get water. Rising out of the water behind him, a Vietcong soldier had seized him and, without mercy, had slit his throat, killing him instantly.

When the chaplain arrived on the scene, he found the Vietcong soldier seated cross-legged on the ground, his arms pinioned behind him, his head pulled back by one of his captors. A distraught company commander, sobbing with grief and rage, held a pistol to his enemy's head. As the chaplain pieced together the story, fellow soldiers urged their commander to take revenge and "waste this miserable animal."

The chaplain knew what he had to do. But, as he described it, he seemed frozen to the spot. For a moment, he couldn't move, couldn't speak. He wanted to turn away and let it happen — just so he didn't have to *see* it happen! After all, this enemy deserved to die, didn't he?

Then, praying silently, he approached the commander. "Sir, you can't do this," he heard himself saying. The officer turned on him, sobbing and screaming in his grief and anger. Then, again, the chaplain spoke in a quiet voice, "Sir, you can't do this."

The commander turned from his prisoner, threw his pistol to the ground, and walked away, sobbing. The prisoner was taken away for interrogation. The crisis was over.

An Important Role

This true story illustrates the chaplain's role as the *conscience* of ministry, when chaplains are assigned to military or naval units or to ships of the line, they are expected to minister to and meet the needs of *all* members of that command. This is why there is great emphasis on continuing education in various pastoral skills within the chaplaincies.

• *Combat duties.* Regardless of the effectiveness of ministry in peacetime, it is in combat that the true value of the chaplain is revealed. Combat tests the limits of human endurance and quickly brings soldiers, sailors, airmen, and marines back to the basic, essential questions of life. In a life-threatening environment of maximum stress, opportunities for life-changing ministry are limited only by the chaplain's physical endurance and spiritual stamina. It is for this reason that chaplains undergo the same rigorous training and must

the unit, speaking with the *authority* of a prophet of the Lord. The chaplain had to settle the questions of conscience with himself before the event. After the fact would have been too late.

Military regulations not only permit but actually require chaplains to be the conscience of the command. While chaplains are under authority in the military services and are expected to obey lawful orders, they also represent and must communicate what God says about the actions of human beings prone to sinful actions. Therefore, soldiers look to chaplains for guidance on matters of conscience. Chaplains exercise spiritual authority while serving under secular authority.

Military chaplains are protected by regulation from performing any act at variance with the tenets of their faith. Since they are noncombatants with special recognition under the Geneva Conventions, they do not bear arms. They can assist the wounded, but they are not expected to participate in offensive operations, except to the extent that they are a part of the military unit engaged in the offensive.

A Continual Duty

Decisions about when to speak out are not confined only to wartime or combat situations. The chaplain will be confronted with this challenge sooner or later in peacetime. The chaplain must raise the moral banner — through lifestyle, speech, sermons, counseling — *before* a crisis, however. This is absolutely essential. Seeking redress *after* the fact (unless the actions were taken without the chaplain's knowledge) is invariably treated as griping, and the chaplain loses credibility.

The conflict between authority and conscience will always be with us. When military chaplains take the courageous route and raise issues of conscience before the fact, and when they speak with the authority of Almighty God, they usually have little difficulty with the authority of men.

—James A. Edgren

maintain the same level of physical fitness as the service members to whom they minister. They must also concentrate on maintaining themselves in a high state of spiritual readiness, so that they are prepared to carry on a dynamic ministry in a combat environment.

Chaplains must have worked through the issues of conscience and the whole spectrum of arguments on the question of bearing arms. They should be well versed in just-war theory and be able to provide assistance to service members who struggle with these issues.

While chaplains need not endorse uncritically the actions of commanders or troops in a combat situation, they are a part of the military establishment being paid with public funds and have taken an oath of office, just as line officers have. They must, therefore, be pre-

---

Morale and Family Concerns

Chaplain ministry in the armed services takes place in the environment of the total institution. In the civilian world, there is a certain "apartness" of the church from the community it serves. This is not so in the military. The chaplain eats, sleeps, and trains with his or her congregation.

The chaplain also is one person in a larger leadership team, and this leadership team is ultimately concerned with the fulfillment of the unit's mission. Anything that detracts from training and completion of the mission is of interest to the command. If a member of the military community worries about family or experiences family problems, the motivation for fulfilling the unit's mission will be hampered. Since the person in tune with the difficulties and morale of the troops is the chaplain, commanding officers expect chaplains either to assist in the resolution of family problems or to refer matters to the proper agency.

A Proactive Approach

Although the command expects the chaplain to be involved with families, a basic motivation for such action is the chaplain's personal understanding of ministry. Stresses from separations, long periods of training, and living with the threat of war—all make the family a logical place of entry for the chaplain. Rather than being reactive, chaplains need to be proactive in this work. The following suggestions will assist the chaplain in ministry to families.

• *Become active in the command's family-support program.* Deployed units appoint representatives in the community to assist during the service member's absence. Given various names—ombudsman, key volunteers—these are people with whom the chaplain needs to develop a positive, supportive relationship. Contact with these unit representatives is vital not only when stateside but also

pared to be a part of a military action that may bring death and destruction upon an enemy of their nation. Chaplains who are uncertain about their feelings on this issue can exercise the option of resigning their commissions and separating themselves from the armed forces *before* entry into combat. Even in combat, chaplains are expected to challenge and confront immoral or unethical actions, and they have a history of having done so.

• *Leadership duties.* Chaplains must exercise moral and spiritual leadership in a military society increasingly hostile to the gospel. How do they do this? The key to the whole process is the word *service.* Chaplains are expected to take the lead when it comes to making the hard choices on moral, ethical, and spiritual issues. In fact, the chap-

---

while deployed. This link is crucial to building chaplain rapport and opening avenues for ministry.

• *Address the stresses of the military lifestyle.* As an institution, the military says both "We care for you" and "The mission comes first." The service member is subject to frequent short-term separations from spouse and family as well as multiple home relocations. While each branch of service has developed a Family Support Program, the chaplain within the individual unit must be particularly sensitive to such issues, developing unit activities that will assist personnel in transitions, in marital communication, and in independent living. Priority goes to predeployment and return programs that address the dynamics of military lifestyle. Parenting programs that teach the skills of communication and discipline are essential for ministry to the whole family.

• *Take special interest in the single-parent family.* Units now include people who are attempting to rear children alone. For these individuals, field training and deployments are potential crisis experi-

ences. Chaplains can assist by keeping up-to-date listings of competent weekly daycare providers and helping to make arrangements for child care during deployment. The pure fatigue of a single parent is the touch point for significant ministry.

• *Acknowledge your vital role within the institution.* Chaplains often leave the programs suggested here to the Family Services Center of the command. Such an approach fails to acknowledge who the chaplain is. The chaplain represents both the command and a particular faith group. Is the faith community's message relevant to any of the above concerns? Can strength from a person's faith assist in meeting the stresses of military life?

While a chaplain can bring many resources to bear in meeting the problems of military lifestyle, his or her role within the system points beyond the mundane to an eternal faith relationship with God. Abdicating our responsibility to meet family needs means limiting our witness to the power of God to feed hungry souls.

—Gerald T. Richards

lain can and will provide a true service when he or she assists the commander in making the right choices.

The chaplain's effectiveness in communicating God's Word to this unique segment of society is directly related to how creative he or she is in ministry. Although the military community has accepted the chaplaincy as a fact of life, for many within that community, the chaplain is irrelevant. The challenge is to rise above that image and conduct a ministry that provides real answers to real problems, demonstrating that the gospel meets needs and that the Christian life is exciting.

In a world in which clergy from many backgrounds are falling into moral impurity, chaplains must set and maintain high moral standards. Even if they never voice it, superiors, colleagues, and subordinates have the highest expectations for chaplains in terms of conduct. They watch the chaplain's lifestyle closely and expect a godly presence that reflects light in a dark world. At the same time there will be pressure to conform, to laugh at dirty jokes, to join in debasement of the opposite sex. Resisting that temptation is absolutely essential to effective ministry.

Chaplains have insider status in a way that most civilian clergy do not. They are a part of the organization by regulation and by law. They have both the right and duty to participate in the policy-making and decision-making processes. Though some commanders may attempt to deny chaplains their seat at the table, relegating their program and input to the periphery, wise commanders will ensure that chaplains are really heard. Chaplains themselves must aggressively work at maintaining their leadership status.

The expectation that chaplains will speak prophetically to the institution is foreign to bureaucratic thinking: Let the chaplain sermonize and give guidance, counsel, and comfort to the religious, but God forbid that he or she should influence policy or have any impact on the decision-making process! This prevalent point of view reveals a misunderstanding of the chaplain's role.

Nathan the prophet could say to King David "Thou art the man!" because he had access to the king. He had won the right to be heard because, as a prophet of God, he regularly spoke to the institution with a prophetic voice.

Governmental and Popular Support

The military chaplaincy is deeply rooted in the constitutional and statutory foundations of our country and has, from the earliest days, enjoyed popular support by our people. Congress appropriates public funds year by year to support the service chaplaincies and their programs. These funds pay salaries, build chapels and religious-education facilities, provide equipment and transportation, and buy Bibles, hymnbooks and religious-education materials. In addition, public funds pay for conferences, training programs, retreats, and professional development for chaplains and assistants. The three chaplain schools are also publicly funded.

Chaplains Funds (offerings given in chapels) are used to supplement public funding and "to meet [the] social needs of the religious community." Receiving of offerings is also viewed as an integral part of worship. As a result, it is not unusual for military chapels to give 15 to 25 percent of their income to charitable, humanitarian, and missionary enterprises outside the military establishment.

The chaplaincies of the three armed services are established and defined in public law (Title 10, United States Code). This statutory authority confers an official status upon military chaplains within the federal government that is unique in American public life. In no other sector are chaplains as firmly established. Although this official status of the chaplaincy has been challenged in court (most recently and notably in the case of Katcoff v. Marsh [1979–1986]), the courts have consistently upheld the constitutionality of the military chaplaincies. The first amendment of the Constitution prohibits enactment of any law "respecting the establishment of religion or prohibiting the free exercise thereof." In striking a balance between the "establishment" and the "free exercise" clauses, Congress has recognized the necessity of the chaplaincy to protect and enhance the "free exercise" rights of service members. At the same time, chaplains are trained to avoid even the appearance of any "establishment" of religion. Yet, Congress has, in essence, allowed for limited establishment in order to protect individual religious rights.

In recent years there has been increasing pressure from various segments of society to eliminate the chaplaincies or to at least cut back their public funding severely. So far the military chaplaincies have survived these attacks. However, as this nation becomes more secular in character, it will become increasingly necessary to justify the chaplaincy. That can be done, though, as long as chaplains continue to provide quality ministry in the toughest of environments. As they do, the chaplaincies will no doubt survive and thrive.

—James A. Edgren

30

Hospital Chaplains

Throughout its history the church has held in high esteem those who compassionately minister to the sick. Of course, Scripture clearly encourages such ministry. In Matthew 25 we hear Jesus saying, "I was sick, and you looked after me. . . . I tell you the truth, whatever you did for one of the least of these brothers of mine, you did for me." Though reaching out to the sick is a supreme act of love worthy of every pastor's time and energy, this special form of ministry presents difficult challenges, demands a solid sense of personal identity, and requires a specific set of purposes.

Challenges

The hospital has been and will continue to be a fertile field for Christian ministry. However, the very nature of the hospital has changed, making effective ministry somewhat more difficult. Consider:

• *The rapid change of the hospital.* After World War II, government subsidy programs helped fund hospital construction, and many new hospitals were built. Federal expenditures for research also expanded — from $73 million in 1950 to over $2 billion in 1972. As a result, technology advanced dramatically. As Medicare and Medicaid were incorporated into social security, the best medical care became more available to everyone, regardless of socioeconomic status.

Recently, DRGs (diagnosis related groups) and their reported rates have become a large determining factor in treatment plans. If a hospital can find a way to treat a patient for less money than the specific rate of reimbursement designated by a DRG, it can keep the difference as profit. If the hospital's treatment occasionally costs more than the designated reimbursement, it absorbs the loss.

The trend appears, therefore, to have been a move away from the more personal care that was available years ago. Most observers see a movement toward larger, perhaps more impersonal facilities, where patients may suffer greater feelings of anonymity. Many hospitals have become serious about making a profit and being cost driven. Today's chaplain enters an environment in which hospital managers may be more financially motivated than service motivated.

● *The inner tension of the chaplain.* What is the chaplain's role and responsibility in the midst of all of this change? Lawrence Holst describes the tension a chaplain faces when he or she attempts to minister within two worlds, the worlds of religion and medicine. We can readily identify the source of the tension. The chaplain, often being an ordained minister, usually has specialized training as a pastor in the context of a local church. This pastor then becomes a chaplain and is thrust into a foreign, highly specialized medical field that uses a distinct vocabulary and delivers a unique set of problems.

The chaplain identifies with both worlds, yet does not feel entirely at home in either. Chaplains are an enigma to both worlds: Medicine does not consider them "medical enough" and questions their relevance; the church often does not consider them "pastoral enough," questioning their essential identity and calling. But despite the tensions and enigmas, the hospital chaplain can be very much committed to both worlds and can serve as a vital link between them (Holst 1985, 12–27).

● *The complex environment of the ministry.* In visiting the sick, then, the minister encounters a unique and challenging environment for ministry. People involved with illness, both patients and patients' families, need so many things on so many levels. Almost everyone at this time desires spiritual counsel and encouragement.

Patients and their loved ones are often more open to considering spiritual truths during a physical crisis. Granted, sometimes this openness is motivated by pure fear over the current situation or extenuating circumstances, yet the opportunity to draw near in ministry is still present and valid. For patients and patients' families alike, a time of sickness encourages evaluation of life's past choices and future plans. Priorities and schedules are challenged and will often be reevaluated. People make significant decisions, charting new courses of action for the future.

As a patient evaluates decisions and contemplates choices, the chaplain often has a unique opportunity to help guide the process. The chaplain also has an unparalleled opportunity to demonstrate God's love and concern.

Identity

What kind of person ministers effectively in the hospital? In today's technological society, the pastor and chaplain must have a sure sense of personal identity. Apart from some specific techniques, strong Christian character is the crucial requirement for developing and maintaining that identity. Three Bible passages give insight into these traits: 2 Corinthians 5:20, Luke 10:30–37, and 2 Corinthians 1:3–4. According to these passages, a chaplain must be:

• *One who can represent Christ in a secular environment.* In 2 Corinthians 5:20, Paul writes that we are "ambassadors for Christ." An ambassador speaks on behalf of the sovereign who sent him or her, and it is the duty of the ambassador to proclaim faithfully and accurately the sovereign's message. In a real sense, therefore, it can be said that the message of the ambassador *is* the message of the sovereign.

All believers should serve as Christ's ambassadors, whether in the marketplace, a recreational area, or the hospital. By the nature of our relationship with Christ, we are automatically identified with him, and our actions and words are a direct reflection upon him.

As a minister for Jesus Christ enters the hospital environment, his or her responsibility as ambassador does not automatically go on hold or into remission because of entering a secular institution. Ambassadors for Jesus Christ are ambassadors no matter where they happen to be at the moment. Often the sufferer is looking for a word from God and is trying to make some sense out of his or her pain, waiting for God's ambassador to help. Christ's ambassador, through words and actions, can function as the hands and mouth of Jesus in a powerful, incarnational form of ministry.

• *One who can show mercy to all.* In response to the question "Who is my neighbor?" Jesus told the story of the Good Samaritan in Luke 10:30–37. On the surface, we might understand Jesus as teaching that a person should always help others in need. However, in light of the context of Jesus' rejection, we could view this parable as a reflection of his own ministry. Jesus, like the Samaritan, was the outcast one who was nevertheless willing to seek and save people who were perishing. Whether one looks at the surface interpretation or views the passage as a reflection of Jesus' ministry, the message remains that we are to "go and do the same." A chaplain should be able to demonstrate compassion and mercy freely.

What does it mean to behave like a compassionate and merciful neighbor? What are we do to? The Good Samaritan felt compassion for the man along the road and therefore he responded. Compassion calls for sympathy, understanding, patience, and sensitivity to those who are underprivileged, sick, or suffering. To show mercy means to give of ourselves willingly and cheerfully.

• *One who can offer comfort based on a close relationship with the Comforter.* The chaplain should also be a comforter of those who suffer. Paul writes in 2 Corinthians 1:3–4, "Praise be to the God and Father of our Lord Jesus Christ, the Father of compassion and the God of all comfort, who comforts us in all our troubles, so that we can comfort those in any trouble with the comfort we ourselves have received from God." All Christians experience affliction. Probably no one experienced more afflictions as a Christian than Paul, who was beaten, stoned, shipwrecked, robbed, and starved (see 2 Cor. 11:23–30). Through all of this, Paul encouraged his readers to shift their perspec-

---

Chaplains and the Health Care Team

Effective hospital ministry requires the ability to function as a member of an interdisciplinary team, working on a daily basis with nurses, physicians, technicians, social workers, and other health care professionals. Chaplains must both demonstrate the need for their place on this team and then function as true professionals among their care-giving peers.

A Needed Ministry

Even though the hospital as a modern institution has blossomed from its Christian roots in monastic hospices, we can no longer assume clergy will be working in health care environments. Pastoral care departments typically fall first to the fiscal axe when budgets tighten. Therefore, hospital chaplains must learn to defend their roles to hospital administrators and medical practitioners, especially if they minister in medical centers unaffiliated with a religious body.

To maintain adequate administrative support, chaplains can regu-larly document the services they provide and the ways the quality of care has improved through chaplaincy ministry. In a sense, chaplains can "market" pastoral care creatively by identifying new areas in which the needs of patients, families, and hospital staff can benefit from pastoral resources. Such marketing involves research, education (of hospital staff and administration), and promotion. For example, research could help establish pastoral ministry as a valued part of hospital services in such areas as pain management, ethics education for medical staff, outpatient care, and the development of various support groups.

A Dual Focus

Chaplains assess and respond to the spiritual needs of patients and their families. Nurses and nursing aids can be most helpful in this ministry, since they interact the most with patients and their families and can provide crucial insights about family dynamics and

tive from the temporal to the eternal (see 2 Cor. 4:17–18). Christians are to keep their eyes focused on Jesus Christ, not upon the temporal things that might steal their attention away from the Lord.

The source of all comfort in the midst of our afflictions is God himself. He is the God of all comfort. Receiving comfort from God during their trials enables the comforted believers to comfort others.

What does it really mean to comfort? The word *comfort* means to impart strength and hope. The original Greek root used in this passage is *paraclete*, which is also used to describe the ministry of the Holy Spirit. The word describes one who stands beside another per-

---

patients' needs. Ideally, all team members consult in weekly interdisciplinary team meetings to develop a care plan related to the physical, emotional, and spiritual aspects of each patient's situation.

Chaplains, however, have a second focus. They not only care for patients and their families but also minister to the medical staff, who typically experience high levels of stress in their work. Research has shown that clergy offer significant support to other members on the health care team, helping to counter burnout. Thus, time spent at the nurses' station listening to and supporting fellow team members is as much a part of hospital ministry as bedside visits with families in crisis. Chaplains may establish support groups for medical staff in critical-care areas, they may conduct grief workshops, or they may offer worship services for hospital staff.

The Necessary Competence

As each profession represented on the health care team performs a different function, members expect each other to be competent in their various fields. A chaplain can en-

hance professional competence in the eyes of colleagues in at least three ways:

• *Learn to communicate special expertise.* Pastors are the experts in spiritual life, ethics, and methods of pastoral care. They must communicate this knowledge and its practical applications to the other team members.

• *Develop objective assessment methods.* Colleagues can be shown that the chaplain is not just dealing in subjective generalities. A chaplain can demonstrate empirical assessment by using detailed evaluation forms or inventories. See, for instance, George Fitchett's *Spiritual Assessment in Pastoral Care: A Guide to Selected Resources* (Decatur, Ga.: JPC Publications, 1993).

• *Become familiar with the technical side of health care.* To work effectively with other caregivers, a chaplain must become thoroughly conversant with the terminology of medical diagnosis and treatment. The challenge is to work professionally within the relationship that exists among theology, medicine, and the behavioral sciences, without losing one's identity and profile as a minister of the gospel.

—*Frank Milstead Woggon*

son to encourage him or her when that person is undergoing severe testing. The Holy Spirit as Paraclete strengthens and guides us, comforts and consoles us (see John 14:16, 26; 15:26). Likewise, when we minister to others who are suffering, we go to them in order to stand beside them, comforting and encouraging them during their time of need.

Purpose

The ministry of the hospital chaplain is broad and can be wonderfully rewarding. To the chaplain, the patients become a mission field, and the hospital staff becomes a congregation. Ministry takes place when divine resources touch human needs through loving channels, to the glory of God. This is possible when the chaplain is clear about his or her specific purposes and roles:

Dealing with Death

Chaplains are considered the death, bereavement, and grief experts on the health care team. Yet death in the modern hospital is a medical pronouncement and ideally should be announced to the family by the physician. The chaplain can coach the physician on how to break the news and can pick up the pieces and shepherd the family after the physician is gone.

Good Grief

To minister effectively with grieving people, we must be convinced grief is essentially therapeutic rather than pathologic, and "the best way out is through." It's important to get the bereaved into a private space where wailing and screaming will not be upsetting to other families. Any strong expression of grief—short of doing violence to oneself or others, or tearing up the premises—is permissible.

All the tasks surrounding death in the hospital, such as contacting relatives, choosing a funeral home, and discussing organ donation, potentially contribute to good grieving. In cases of infant death, for example, naming and holding the dead baby can help bereaved parents move through denial to the acceptance of reality and the experience of its pain.

Chaplains help to bring closure to the immediate bereavement experience by gathering the family around the deceased, inviting all to join hands, and reciting a psalm or leading a prayer of thanksgiving for the life of the deceased and for passage to God's safekeeping.

First Facing Death

Chaplains can spend years in training, learning techniques and methods for dealing with the dying and counseling the bereaved. No

• *To provide pastoral care for patients.* The primary thrill of the chaplaincy comes from working directly with patients. The staff chaplain makes daily rounds and is available 24 hours a day to offer spiritual counseling and emotional support to the sick, recovering, and dying patient. A normal day includes not only daily rounds, but also visitation of patients who are scheduled for surgery the next day.

Making rounds involves visiting patients who have recently been admitted into the hospital. The chaplain is clinically trained in making effective calls in these situations. The techniques used to enter into conversation with a patient vary, but the goal is always to be an ambassador for Jesus Christ, offering personal availability for ministry in ways the patient might request.

The chaplain will find patients dealing with grief, joy, fear, anxiety, or any other emotion. Specific problems range from the evident physical ones to financial and marital concerns. Any problem that a

---

amount of training, however, can take the place of the one foundational prerequisite that will determine the true effectiveness of those who wish to minister compassionately to the bereaved: thoroughly confronting one's own mortality.

Here are some key steps involved in that process:

• *Make a will.* Contemplating your death and what will become of your possessions powerfully confronts you with your own mortality.

• *Compose care directives.* Think through how much treatment you would want should you be dying, and document this in a living will. Stipulate the person you would want to serve as surrogate decision-maker for you in the event you become unable to speak for yourself.

• *Draft a list of the ten persons or things you value most* and prioritize them. Imagine losing them one at a time, from the least to the greatest. Write your feelings and thoughts upon contemplating each loss.

• *Fill out a hospital Report of Death on yourself.* This would include information such as the hour, day, month, and year you imagine you will die; the cause of death; the identity of the next of kin; and the funeral home or crematory to which you expect to be released.

• *Observe an autopsy.*

• *Identify the three greatest losses you have experienced in life.* Recall your feelings and thoughts in great detail. Let your emotions open up to the pain of loss in your own life.

• *Write "To be opened only on the event of my death" letters* to your most significant others and place the letters in your safe-deposit box.

• *Write instructions about your funeral* or memorial service that you want your survivors to follow.

• *Say your "I love you's" today to those who need to hear them.* Christopher Morley once said that if we all suddenly learned we had only five minutes left to live, every phone booth in the country would be filled with people blurting out, "I love you!" Why wait until the last five minutes?

—*Wayne Willis*

pastor would face in a pastor's study, the chaplain will face in the hospital room; however, in the hospital the problem is accented by the patient's physical trauma.

If a patient has no minister from home, the chaplain serves as friend and pastoral figure, providing neutral ground for discussion of spiritual matters. The chaplain may not be the patient's continuing pastor but can still provide God's perspective during a needy time.

The primary tools available for the chaplain's use are good listening techniques, Scripture, and prayer. Listening, sharing a verse of Scripture, and praying helps bring fractured lives back into focus. A good chaplain is able to maintain a proper balance between inviting consideration of the eternal perspective and dealing practically with temporal reality.

• *To offer support to patients' families.* Sometimes the patient is in no condition to speak with a chaplain. During those visits, the chaplain focuses on the patient's family, being available for calls to the emergency room, intensive-care unit, and surgical waiting areas to help with the distressed family of a critically ill or dying patient.

In this ministry, the chaplain can provide crisis counseling and support. This is an exciting and rewarding ministry. Deep and lasting friendships often develop between the chaplain and family as the chaplain provides guidance and directs attention toward the One who is able to provide stability in the midst of instability.

• *To serve as pastor for the care-giving staff.* The chaplain is able to be, in an often stressful and demanding environment, an understanding friend and confidant with a sympathetic listening ear. Staff members who do not have a minister of their own often seek the chaplain's counsel, especially during times of personal and family need. Whereas the average stay of a patient is only four days in an acute-care hospital, the staff member may remain in the hospital for years. Chaplains should therefore seek to develop long-term ministry with the personnel working in all areas of the facility on all three shifts.

The chaplain, working in cooperation with the care-giving team, can also serve on a bioethics committee, counsel in the chemical-dependency unit, make rounds with the oncology team, and supply crisis counseling during emergency-room trauma. These contacts open ample opportunities to meet, encourage, and pastor an often stressed-out staff.

• *To function as a liaison for local clergy.* The hospital chaplain typically sees a patient before his or her own minister is aware that hospitalization has occurred. With the patient's permission, the chaplain can call the family pastor, priest, rabbi, or other spiritual leader. The chaplain then remains available and ready to provide pastoral care until the patient's minister arrives. In this ministry, the chaplain serves as an arm of the local pastor's ministry. When chaplains build a foundation of trust with the local clergy, they will be genuinely appreciated for this transitional role. It is exciting to see shepherding members of the body of Christ working together.

• *To do public-relations work for the hospital.* Chaplains often serve as the hospital's religious-community public-relations person. This ministry includes coordinating any services that might be held in the hospital, providing pulpit supply for vacationing pastors, or acting as community-resource person on topics such as hospital visitation, terminal illness, death, and the grieving process. This ministry calls the chaplain to function as a minister-at-large for the community. Funeral services and other public duties often fall to the community chaplain when a family has nowhere else to turn.

The thrill of the chaplaincy flows from being uniquely involved when a sufferer experiences fresh awareness of the greatness of God's grace. To encourage that miracle, chaplains rush into emergency rooms late at night to stand with the loved ones of those seriously injured. They minister amid all the tubes and equipment of life-support systems. And they stand at the graveside, comforting the grieving, before driving back to the hospital to smile and congratulate a proud new father. It is to these godly, humble, untrumpeted servants of the Lord that Christ will say, "Well done."

—*Douglas M. Cecil*

Resources

Holst, L. 1985. Hospital ministry: The role of the chaplain today. New York: Crossroad.

The hospital chaplain: A training manual for instructors and chaplains-in-training. 1987. Anaheim, Cal.: Hospital Chaplains' Ministry of America.

31

Prison Chaplains

Over 1.2 million men and women are locked up in the jails and prisons of our nation today. Constituting only 5 percent of the world's population, we Americans incarcerate over 50 percent of the world's prisoners. Our prisons are full and desperately overcrowded, and as quickly as we build new ones, we cannot keep up with the need for more beds and cells. The demand for ever-increasing prison space is fueled both by a rising crime rate and by the fact that between 60 and 70 percent of those released from prison commit new crimes within four years.

Before we become overwhelmed by statistics like these, we must step back and consider how the power of the gospel can make a difference in our prisons through the critical ministry of prison chaplains. We might begin by asking these four basic questions: What is a prison for? What does a prison chaplain actually do? What are the special challenges of chaplain ministry? And how can a congregation fit in with chaplain ministry?

Places for Repentance and Restoration

Our Savior's pointed words in Matthew 25 about involvement with people who are hurting, destitute, or locked away in jails has throughout history generated Christian concern for the prisoner. Though often thought of as places for punishment, prisons do not have to serve this primary role. In the eighteenth century, for example, Pope Pius IX organized a papal prison for juveniles, placing them in individual cells for the purpose of spiritual reflection, not for punishment.

The Quakers in 1772 built a prison in Philadelphia—the Walnut Street Jail—taking punishment off the streets and placing offenders in private cells so they could meditate and repent of their sins. Here the name "penitentiary" was used to express a philosophy of redemption and restoration, not merely retribution and strict justice. A chaplain was employed in the Walnut Street Jail to address the spiritual needs of those imprisoned. As the American prison system evolved through periods of what can only be viewed today as incredible brutality, the role of chaplain gained considerable significance.

Today there are basically three different levels in our criminal justice system, and each has its unique dynamics and ministry challenges. The upper level consists of the Federal Bureau of Prisons, a federal agency with over 70 institutions housing over 83,000 prisoners at present. This prison system has a more sophisticated clientele, in general, than the state systems'. The federal determinate-sentencing law means that federal prisoners will be serving longer sentences and more of their sentenced time. With a high level of educational qualifications required for all of its personnel, these prisons usually employ chaplains from mainline (or at least the larger) denominations.

The middle level is the state prison systems. Each state has its own body of laws and often its own correctional culture. Many of the state systems have death rows and house a larger number of violent inmates. Penal philosophies vary widely from state to state. Today, some states, implementing rugged cost-cutting measures, are exploring cutting back on chaplaincy services or at least moving them to a contract status outside of the prison structure. This is a cause for concern in the ranks of chaplains and could seriously affect the delivery of religious services to inmate populations.

At the lower level of criminal justice stands the network of county and city jails where inmates are either serving relatively short sentences or awaiting trial. The dynamics in these institutions are quite different from those of a prison. Often the men and women housed in these institutions are reeling from the first shock of losing jobs and income, trying to cope with all the attendant trauma to their families as car and house payments come to a stop. These men and women typically have their families and roots in the local community and, therefore, church members can have a powerful outreach to their own neighbors in these local jails.

Many prisoners go through these various criminal justice systems feeling discouraged, angry, bitter, and totally rejected. Prison tends to make them dependent and often leaves them unprepared for life in society when they get out. Learning to survive in a violent prison culture with its unique codes of morality, and facing a perceived rejection by society, few prisoners become more functional on the outside world as a result of supposed "rehabilitation" on the inside.

A Ministry of Uncommon Compassion

From a spiritual perspective, a prison is one of the great bastions of the Evil One, a place where men and women are shackled in the chains of hopelessness and despair, violence and hatred, and all the attendant negative emotions. Yet it can also be a place of tremendous opportunity, where men and women meet the person of Jesus Christ and his loving acceptance. This can take place in a setting where, perhaps for the first time, people have significant time to think, to study, and to act on their new spiritual insights.

Standing in the gap, holding out the possibility of this incredible inner transformation for those so long without hope, is the small band of prison chaplains. These men and women have committed their lives to that difficult ministry of bringing the Good News of God's grace into our penal institutions. Today the office of prison chaplain is well established, even while its job description and philosophy is constantly changing to meet the growing complexities of the correctional field. It is a ministry in one of the most demanding and stressful fields of service, yet it is so little understood by the average church member. What in particular do prison chaplains actually do?

The opportunities for different forms of ministry can be almost overwhelming in terms of time and numbers. At the most basic level, the chaplain schedules regular times for worship and Bible study, led by both the chaplain and outside volunteers. In addition, individual and group counseling sessions provide opportunities for the chaplain to hear prisoners' concerns and problems, while often confronting their attitudes and lifestyles.

A chaplain's work almost always includes meetings with inmates to notify them of family emergencies, severe illnesses, and deaths. He or she makes the necessary arrangements required by these crisis situations. Often these emergencies—always traumatic—are even more so for those who are locked up and feeling utterly helpless.

Another area of responsibility for the busy chaplain is the management and coordination of outside ministries and programs for prisoners. These ministries bring tremendous and welcome resources to the religious program in a jail or prison. They expand and multiply the ministry of the chapel-related community far beyond the capabilities of a full-time chaplaincy staff, and they reach into the rest of the prison population, as well. Such resources include many different kinds of programs: evangelistic crusades, marriage seminars, preaching missions, and concerts.

On the downside, however, chaplains know that each outside program demands tedious and meticulous preparation and planning, placing an added burden of security measures on the correctional staff. This management of the volunteer program is a demanding task, one that is seldom appreciated or understood by outside ministries.

Special Problems in Prison Ministry

The chaplain's work can bring deep satisfaction. Being a primary source of comfort, hope, and personal acceptance to those who so desperately need it is certainly one reward. It's also gratifying to know that one is working with the kinds of people with whom the Savior spent so much of his own time, with those who are hurting and those who do not fit easily into our church culture. Christ's habit of working with these kinds of people was what caused so much consternation and uproar in the Jewish religious community of his day.

Christian Rehabilitation

What does it mean for a prisoner to be truly rehabilitated in Christ? Only God knows the heart of an individual, but we in the church can have God's heart as we reach out to prisoners and support the work of the prison chaplain. This ministry demands an abundance of discernment, common sense, nurturing ability, and patience.

Difficult Distinctions

Prison ministry is difficult. Anyone who reaches out to prisoners with the gospel must be cautious and wise, recognizing that true rehabilitation springs from a radical change of heart. There is little behind a prison's stark concrete walls and cold bars that can accomplish lasting change other than a genuine encounter with Jesus Christ.

Here are some recommendations for pastors or church members assisting the prison chaplain.

• *Discern the truth in behaviors.*
Is the conversion real, or is the prisoner just faking it? Is it true rehabilitation or simply a "jailhouse conversion"? Naturally, we must be alert to the reality of manipulation; some prisoners will mimic evangelical jargon that we call "church talk." The one true indication of conversion is Christlike behavior, and not returning to crime is the most compelling evidence of rehabilitation.

• *Use common sense in giving.*
Avoid giving a prisoner material goods, such as money and stamps, and avoid having an ex-offender move in with a church family just after release. These practices often are a violation of prison policy and can lead to victimization.

Working with the prisoner or ex-offender will sometimes require making hard decisions and being confrontational in love. Simply giving in to every request for money, materials, or other assistance is not good for the prisoner or the church.

At the same time, there are also significant problems and difficulties for anyone involved in this ministry. Here are just four of the unique problems prison chaplains face:

• *Struggling with mountains of paperwork.* Because of the security problems inherent in such a climate of restraint, there is an almost endless flow of paperwork to be done. Time and energy for direct ministry with persons seems constantly drained into the writing, signing, and filing of countless reports. How frustrating!

• *Watching "successes" walk out the door.* The people who excel in spiritual growth often become a parish pastor's strongest supporters, moving into Christian service and taking up positions of leadership in the congregation. For a chaplain, the greatest people successes are the first to leave the prison and never come back. Unless they get into

---

• *Offer biblical nurture in abundance.* Make sure the prisoner's conversion is built on a solid biblical foundation and visit regularly to conduct in-prison Bible studies. A conversion that emanates from a knowledge of God through the Scriptures has a better chance of being genuine than a spontaneous decision rooted in the emotion of a prison chapel service.

Occasionally it may be appropriate to have an ex-offender give his or her testimony in the local church, but avoid the temptation of a speaking circuit that puts ex-offenders in a spotlight. They should not be given a responsible position in the church, either, until there is enduring evidence of growth.

Do create mentoring relationships, though. One of the best ways to stabilize the Christian life of an ex-offender is to get him or her into a strong discipling relationship with a mature Christian. Accountability rooted in biblical principles can lead to genuine rehabilitation.

• *Be patient in viewing slow progress.* The longer someone has been in prison, the more emotional baggage he or she carries. Prisoners often come from dysfunctional families, and their complicated problems have developed over a long period. Simply stated, when working with prisoners and ex-offenders, we will often experience "two steps forward and one step back." Though the negative effects of long-term incarceration may frequently surface, our gentleness and patience will develop a trust relationship that can help heal the wounds.

Several years ago a church pastor told me, "We tried prison ministry once, but it didn't work." He told of bringing an ex-offender into the church who had then apparently stolen a member's watch. Of course, anyone coming into that church could have been a thief. If we are looking for reasons to label people or to eject them from our communities, we will find them. May we see instead the great potential for good that God has built into every human being (Eph. 2:10).

—Don Smarto

some kind of prison ministry, they'll try to forget the painful memories associated with the prison experience and will seldom be heard from again.

 • *Working under secular values.* Pastors' supervisors almost always share in their vision for ministry and espouse similar values. The supervisors of chaplains, however, too often hold a different set of values, viewing chaplains' work from a thoroughly secular perspective.

 • *Feeling like a loner.* Chaplains are often misunderstood by their denominational peers, who have difficulty relating to the kinds of concerns with which prison chaplains wrestle daily. Their work is usually done behind the scenes and out of the spotlight, unrecognized by the community on the outside. Their spouses typically are minimally involved in the work of the prison or jail chapel. A chaplain's

---

Prisoners' Families

How can the local church bring aid and comfort to prisoners' families? We in church leadership might first identify the chaplain of a local jail or prison and then give that person visibility in the church. For example, we might bring him or her to the church to speak, or display a photograph of the chaplain along with those of our foreign missionaries. This will pave the way for a good working relationship between chaplain and church.

Supporting the Chaplaincy

The church can be supportive of the chaplain's work with prisoner families as he or she cares for the spouse and children during the prisoner's incarceration. This relationship works best when the church determines to work within the rules and policies of the institution and accepts the chaplain's limitations on involvement. Specifi-cally, here are guidelines for those becoming involved with prisoners' families:

 •*Respect the chaplain's authority.* Never go around or over the chaplain to implement any form of ministry. We may know the warden, sheriff, or an elected politician who can exert influence on the chaplain, but the chaplain is the pastor of the prison, and the Christian inmates are his or her congregation. We must work with and through the chaplains, respecting their authority.

 • *Help the chaplain follow policy.* The chaplain is a part of the administrative team of the facility, and he or she is aware that the first obligation of the prison is secure custody. Therefore, we must not pressure a chaplain into making exceptions in policy.

For example, we should avoid asking for special favors, such as visitations at unreasonable hours, which would be burdensome to cor-

family often has its own involvement in a local congregation, leaving the chaplain with a vague sense of rejection, or at least a sense of detachment from the church community with which he or she was once involved.

How the Local Church Fits In

Prisoners have been intentionally separated from society at large. As Christians, however, we must never separate members of Christ's body from brothers and sisters in the church. The daunting challenge of chaplaincy is to make the connection between the two communities in every possible way, within the obvious restrictions.

So how can chaplains most effectively work with the church? Con-

---

rectional staff. Do not ask the chaplain to give a prisoner unauthorized books, cakes, clothes, or other materials that are usually restricted. Also, do not pressure chaplains into becoming advocates for a prisoner's case or lure them into a situation in which they must become a character witness on the prisoner's behalf at a hearing or trial. This can create a serious role conflict.

• *Work through established programs.* Two programs that help prisoners' families are the Prison Fellowship Angel Tree Program and the Salvation Army. At Christmas, the Angel Tree Program helps buy gifts for the children of inmates (the incarcerated parent signs the card to the child). Several Salvation Army programs give gifts, food, and clothes to prisoners' families.

• *Don't embarrass the spouse.* Often, because of the social stigma of incarceration, the spouse of a prisoner will stop going to church because of embarrassing questions he or she receives. Some spouses even prefer to tell people they are separated or divorced.

This is where the church needs to be especially sensitive. We can invite the prisoner's family not only to a church service but to social activities as well.

• *Offer marriage enrichment.* Over 80 percent of inmate marriages result in divorce. The chaplain and the local pastor working together can help stabilize the marriage through counseling, marriage-enrichment seminars in the facility, and eventual supportive follow-up in the church after the prisoner's release.

• *Don't neglect the children.* The most neglected members of a prisoner's family are the children. The money drain of the trial and incarceration often results in a woman going to work for the first time or even becoming dependent on welfare. If the prison is far from the home, church members could take turns giving family members a ride to the facility for visitation. The church could also consider setting up a car pool for such routine needs as shopping and doctor's visits.

—*Don Smarto*

sider these five suggestions that can help strengthen relationship with the local church, thereby enhancing our mutual ministry:

● *Maintain a special identity and authority.* The chaplain is the legitimate authority in the institutional community. Though they are the gateway to the Christian community in the prison, too often they may be regarded as an obstacle to be overcome or by-passed by those who would bring their ministries directly to prisoners.

Parish pastors who differ from chaplains in tradition or doctrinal convictions must yet honor chaplains for their personal commitment to a demanding ministry. Chaplains dare not let others undermine their work because of differences. If the local church is serious about this kind of outreach ministry, it is essential that the ministry leaders begin with a serious commitment to the spiritual support of the chaplain, including daily intercessory prayer for his or her ministry.

● *Be open to pastoral support and nurture for personal needs.* Chaplains work constantly with people who are trying to build a relationship solely for the purpose of manipulating them for some personal goal. This can produce great stress, and chaplains need the support and nurture of the church to cope. So chaplains need to let pastors get to know them as people.

It's good to spend unstructured time together whenever schedules allow, perhaps away from the institution. The chaplains' job is a relatively lonely one, but they can begin to share their perception of their task in all of its aspects by exploring such questions as: How do I feel about prison residents in general? What is it about my job that excites me as a pastor?

Chaplains can let pastors in on their hopes and dreams for their work. They can speak at churches or groups and share their vision for ministry among prisoners.

As chaplains get to know local pastors, they sometimes receive from them resources such as books, Bibles and New Testaments, and study materials to strengthen their work and program. Also, professional meetings might significantly enrich a chaplain—if he or she can afford to go. Many churches would be happy to supply this need if they were only made aware of it.

● *Gently confront stereotypes and prejudices.* Many church members hold uninformed attitudes toward prisoners and those released. The church community tends to reflect the basic attitudes of society in general toward prisoners and ex-offenders, rather than a scriptural perspective. That attitude of fear and mistrust has always been a problem, just as it was in Jesus' day. As redeemed children of God, we need to remember we have been forgiven of far more than any convicted person has ever been accused of by society.

We in the church should know more about forgiveness than anyone else. Our criminal justice system makes judgments on the basis of behavioral acts. We serve a holy God who has forgiven us not only of the outward actions but of a far greater body of sin, that of our desires and true motives. Our failure to obey the first two commandments— to love the Lord our God with all our heart and mind, and our neighbor as ourselves—is a shortcoming many too easily excuse. Yet, in spite of these unfortunate tendencies, many churches joyfully welcome ex-prisoners into their fellowships.

• *Work together to form support groups.* As churches express the desire to be involved in prison ministry, chaplains can work to form a small group for the support of an ex-prisoner upon release, providing training to these group members and helping them understand the difficult work of maintaining loving accountability and understanding. Particularly in the case of prisoners released without any other kind of support, such a group can identify a place to live, refer to job possibilities, and organize personal support with a clearly defined structure of loving accountability. The first 180 days after release from incarceration can be the most difficult part of the incarceration experience. For a Christian expecting to be accepted by a Christian community upon release, the reality of nonacceptance can be absolutely devastating.

• *Prepare converted prisoners for church membership.* Some prisoners begin taking an active part in the ministry within the institutional setting. The basic ministry goal here is to establish a strong personal relationship with the particular inmate who has made a profession, to disciple him, to prepare him, and to help him make a commitment to the structure of the welcoming church. This preparation on the inside is as valuable and important as the actual experience upon release.

A sad fact is that of those involved in the Christian community in an institution, 90 to 95 percent do not find a church home on the outside after release. A significant church outreach project, then, is to encourage local churches to enhance inside ministry by building a bridge of relationships that will take a prisoner from his or her institution into the fellowship of the local church after release. Such a program, thoughtfully and carefully carried out, will extend a chaplain's ministry beyond the prison walls and create an effect on the church community on the outside.

Various national revivals and awakenings have generated within the church a concern for prison reform. Christians have played a significant role in past efforts to make the institutions of justice more humane and less destructive, more geared toward bringing about true repentance and personal renewal. Any such trend should be supported by believers with diligent work and constant prayer. Men and women reborn into newness of life out of the correctional context can add a richness of experience to the life of any local church body.

—*George Soltau*

Resources

Colson, C., and D. Van Ness. 1989. Convicted: New hope for ending America's crime. Wheaton, Ill.: Crossway.

Costantino, F. 1981. Crimefighter. Orlando: International Prison Ministries.

Pace, D. 1976. A Christian's guide to effective jail and prison ministry. Terrytown, N.Y.: Revell.

Smarto, D. 1987. Justice and mercy. Wheaton, Ill.: Tyndale.

Van Ness, D. 1986. Crime and its victims: What we can do. Downers Grove, Ill.: InterVarsity.

32

Police Chaplains

A re you a priest or a cop?" I must have been asked that question two dozen times an evening while I patrolled the local fair. I cannot fault people's curiosity. After all, I was outfitted like a police officer — badge, portable radio, baton, chemical Mace, handcuffs, and uniform — but I also wore a clerical collar. I typically responded, "I am the police chaplain — a pastor who works with the police department." Most people seemed to like the idea, although a few shook their heads in disbelief.

A chaplain for a police department seems to many a novel idea. However, some police chiefs, street cops, and progressive communities are beginning to recognize the need for a chaplain in today's law enforcement agency. Unfortunately, few departments have chaplains and few pastors have given serious consideration to this field of volunteer ministry. This uncharted territory needs to be mapped.

Who Needs a Police Chaplain?

Police chaplains first minister to the departments they serve. Peace officers occupy a frontline position when it comes to stress and difficulty. The seamy side of life, criticism and hostility, and sometimes even physical abuse constantly barrage police officers. Burnout presents an ever-present risk, divorce is common, and a creeping cynicism pervades their outlook. Feeling misunderstood by most people, cops tend to stick together in a quasiparanoid state of isolation.

Chaplains serve as an outlet for anger and frustrations, and as a rare source of nonpolice thinking. This role in maintaining the mental health of the officers alone justifies the position.

A chaplain serves the police department in guiding conflict resolution, lending the department his or her reputation as a community leader, providing training insights from the social sciences, and standing ready to give spiritual counsel when asked.

Chaplains also minister alongside the department to serve the community. For example, while on patrol or on call, a chaplain often contacts the victims of crime. Mere presence often adds reassurance and comfort at a stressful time. Suspects in custody will often talk to police chaplains freely, and women prisoners especially appreciate the "protective" presence of a chaplain. Family arguments have been known to calm suddenly when a "priest" appears at the door with the cops. Who wants to beat his wife with a priest watching? People will sometimes avail themselves of the chaplain's crisis counseling, while the authority of the police officers may only set them off.

What Is at Stake?

Prior to serving as a police chaplain, a pastor must resolve certain questions:

• *Why am I doing this?* Pastors seeking only thrills and excitement will have more fun at Disneyland. Police work is usually highly routine, and when it gets exciting, the officers need something more than a thrill seeker beside them. A frustrated, would-be cop will make a poor chaplain. Likewise, someone out to prove something about his bravery or masculinity has a poor motive for serving as a police chaplain. The authoritarian personality who enjoys the power of law enforcement will also make a poor cop and a poor chaplain.

Why *am* I doing this? If the answer is to gratify my own needs rather than to serve the department and the community, then I should take a second look. Chaplains must determine to function as servants — always. They certainly should enjoy the service, but service must come first.

• *How do I feel about law enforcement?* A pastor will make a poor chaplain who generally considers cops to be slow-witted, heavy-handed Neanderthals. Such prejudice would render him or her ineffective.

Likewise, potential chaplains must also come to grips with their feelings about the use of force, including deadly force. Is it necessary? Is it legitimate? Romans 13:1–5 is the standard many chaplains fall back on. A police chaplain must consider the police function to be a necessary and legitimate force within the community. Antipolice crusaders might as well stay clear of the police department.

I, personally, decided to carry chemical Mace and a baton because of the potentially dangerous situations I encountered with a solo partner. If order collapsed, I might be his only backup. The decision was made not without some doubt and even conflict, but it had to be made. Fortunately, I never needed to use either defensive weapon.

- *Can I work in this general atmosphere?* A chaplain does not work in a rarefied atmosphere. The language he or she hears, the people encountered, and the things seen may often be of the crudest variety. The chaplain needs to be able to take these factors in stride. The person who cannot abide profanity or who is easily shocked or flustered will have difficulty with police work.

- *How do I feel about myself?* Do I have the maturity to handle the situations I will encounter? Do I have something vital to offer as a Christian chaplain? Can I remain calm in stressful situations? Do I have the courage to face dilemmas and perhaps physical dangers? Can I retain my Christian perspective and my ability to relate to others amid difficult circumstances? Will I be accepting of others, and do I expect the cops to accept me? Do I plan to give the job the time and commitment it will require?

In others words, do I believe I have what it takes to be an effective chaplain? If I have grave doubts, I'll no doubt project them to those around me.

How Do I Prepare?

Once a chaplain is approved for a department, he or she needs extensive orientation. From the beginning the chaplain, to be effective, must have rapport with the chief and the officers below him, and a chaplain needs to maintain an open line of communication with the top administrators.

Riding on patrol with many different officers is indispensable for getting a feel for what it is like for the beat cop out on the streets. As the chaplain begins to feel the stresses, learn the jargon, get comfortable with the procedures, befriend the patrolmen, and catch the style of police work, effectiveness increases considerably.

Becoming known personally and breaking the barriers of suspicion and doubt are crucial. Until the patrolmen trust a chaplain, he or she will be merely someone to babysit. The patrol car proves a marvelous moving arena for conversation and bridge building. Chaplains know that they've found acceptance when patrol officers let them use the radio and start kidding them as mercilessly as their fellow officers. In my case, when the cops' language remained salty around me and I was invited to an off-duty poker party, I knew my orientation was completed.

Beginning chaplains will find reserve officer training at a police academy to be another valuable asset. In some states a minimum class of twenty hours or so may be required, but often one can continue with additional hours to qualify as a full-fledged reserve officer. Classes may be held in evenings for part-time students.

Not every chaplain will have the time or inclination to take significant police training, but the ones who do will find their effectiveness increased. In my case, this reserve-officer training gave me a new edge with the department. They considered me one of them and showed new confidence in me. Knowing their business better gave me a new confidence, too. I considered it far better to be trained for something I hoped never to use than to come up short in some dreadful emergency situation.

Attending departmental training sessions also improves police skills. Camaraderie grows when the chaplain and the officers practice on one another with a baton! It pays to be one with the troops in as many ways as possible.

Continuing education for police chaplains proves more difficult. There are few seminars for police chaplains, although at least one academy near Los Angeles offers a short course. A chaplain can also cull journal articles from such publications as *Police Chief, Journal of Police Science and Administration, Police,* and *Law Enforcement News,* since there is no journal devoted exclusively to chaplains' concerns. Chaplain Bob Turnbull's book *Calling Angel One* provides an interesting look at one chaplain's style.

The International Conference of Police Chaplains also offers information and guidelines for chaplaincy programs. Classes on crisis intervention, psychology, and criminal science also prove useful for practicing chaplains. As in any other professional field, continuing education is essential to improving skills and broadening one's expertise as a police chaplain.

What Is My Role?

Maintaining the role of police chaplain becomes a delicate balancing act. Role pitfalls abound, such as:

• *Supercop.* This is the chaplain trying to "out-cop" the cops. Chaplains must not become so involved in the police game that they forget their role. When a chaplain begins telling the officers how to do their job or becomes overinvolved in the functions a police officer should perform, he or she is forgetting the role. The role is not competitor to the cops. A chaplain is there to learn from them and help them. If the department wanted another patrolman, they would have hired a police officer. A pastor is brought aboard to be a chaplain.

• *Snitch.* Police officers call an informer a "snitch." Nobody really likes snitches, not even the officers. A police chaplain must take pains never to become a snitch, even inadvertently. Confidences simply must remain confidential.

Every department has its personnel disputes, its power plays, its misunderstandings and disagreements, and its rumors. Chaplains become privy to many privileged communications and even more rumors and complaints. Breached confidences will ruin credibility, since the chaplain's effectiveness is pegged to the trust officers have in him or her. Chaplains must learn to remain both neutral and trustworthy in all their dealings with department members.

• *Cynic.* The cynic has also lost role identification. Healthy skepticism keeps a police officer effective — and alive — but skepticism easily slides over into cynicism. Too much dirt and pain and frustration can make a cynic of about anybody. Chaplains must beware, lest overidentification with the police officers robs them of the very thing they have to offer: themselves.

If chaplains become hardened and uncaring, if they lose their perspective, if they begin to divide the world into good guys and bad guys, they need to withdraw and reevaluate their attitudes. Cynics will be of no help as police chaplains.

• *Preacher.* While *preacher* is a marvelous title for parish pastors, it can be a derogatory label for police chaplains. Chaplains with a reputation for preaching to their partners will be ineffective at the very task they attempt to undertake.

Preachers are chaplains who consider the patrol car a pulpit, taking advantage of their captive audience. They ooze platitudes at every opportunity and lecture patrolmen incessantly. Without taking the time to earn the right to be heard, they assume they have a pat answer for every situation. A preacher will be tuned out permanently.

Chaplains do have a relevant message to proclaim — a message of God's love and reconciliation. However, wise chaplains learn to wait until the message is practically drawn out of them by an officer at the proper time. Effective chaplains are heard and do minister, simply because they understand their role and capture the right moment. They learn to separate their Christian function from their service function, and then blend them together when the moment is ripe.

• *Martyr.* Such a chaplain will burn out before he or she has accomplished the task. No chaplain will ever perfect the department and convert every cop. These are just not practical goals. Problems remain, cops hold out, and chaplains feel terribly insignificant at times. The martyr cannot live with this and will destroy himself or herself trying to be a savior.

Yet, while such chaplains incessantly chase sirens, who is with their families? Who is pastoring their churches? Chaplains must pursue realistic expectations and set sane schedules. As in any other ministry, chaplains who do not want to become martyrs must live with their own less-than-perfect efforts.

What Am I Doing out There?

The police chaplain has an interesting and often unique ministry. He may be out on the streets at midnight with a vomiting drunk or in a smoky police lounge talking to a desperate rookie about to lose his job. Sometimes she views the vilest of human motives and other times may witness true human courage. Through routine hours of patrol, to awful moments of stark tragedy, to joyous times of deep brotherhood, the police chaplain ministers. The chaplain is a servant, much as Christ served those around him.

Jesus Christ ministered among people of all kinds. He worked with the tax collectors and harlots and sinners. He took his message and himself out into the world to the places where he found need. The chaplain in the patrol car, in the precinct station, in the dark alleys and wounded homes and seedy bars, the chaplain among the pimps and thieves and wifebeaters and drunks, the chaplain encouraging and supporting the men and women who keep our lives safe — that chaplain is doing the work of Christ. He or she is bringing salt and light to the disheartened and those in the dark.

Police chaplains have two things to offer: themselves, in loving, caring service, and a message of hope and renewal found in the gospel of Jesus Christ. Either of these alone remains inadequate for the situation, but combined together, they have transforming power.

On the doors of the Los Angeles Police Department patrol cars is painted the motto: "To serve and to protect." Across the heart of every police chaplain should be stenciled: "To serve and to protect those who serve and protect."

Police chaplaincy is a high calling in an often-lowly place. While frequently routine, many times frustrating and discouraging, occasionally dangerous, at times hilarious, and only sometimes fulfilling, police chaplaincy is always worthwhile. In serving both the police and the community, the police chaplain serves Christ.

—*James D. Berkley*